Also available from ASQ Quality Press:

Finding the Leader in You: A Practical Guide to Expanding Your Leadership Skills
Anton G. Camarota

Inside Knowledge: Rediscovering the Source of Performance Improvement
David Fearon & Steven A. Cavaleri

Transformational Leadership: Creating Organizations of Meaning
Stephen Hacker and Tammy Roberts

Making Change Work: Practical Tools for Overcoming Human Resistance to Change
Brien Palmer

The Six Sigma Path to Leadership: Observations from the Trenches
David H. Treichler

The Synergy of One: Creating High-Performing Sustainable Organizations through Integrated Performance Leadership
Michael J. Dreikorn

The Quality Improvement Glossary
Donald L. Siebels

Simplified Project Management for the Quality Professional: Managing Small & Medium-size Projects
Russell T. Westcott

Work Overload: Redesigning Jobs to Minimize Stress and Burnout
Frank M. Gryna

To request a complimentary catalog of ASQ Quality Press publications, call 800-248-1946, or visit our Web site at http://qualitypress.asq.org.

Leadership for Results

Removing Barriers to Success for People, Projects, and Processes

Tom Barker, Ph.D.

ASQ Quality Press
Milwaukee, Wisconsin

American Society for Quality, Quality Press, Milwaukee 53203
© 2006 by ASQ Quality Press
All rights reserved. Published 2005
Printed in the United States of America

12 11 10 09 08 07 06 05   5 4 3 2 1

Library of Congress Cataloging-in-Publication Data

Barker, Tom, 1951–
Leadership for results : removing barriers to success for people, projects, and
processes / Tom Barker.
  p. cm.
Includes bibliographical references and index.
ISBN 0-87389-669-6 (soft cover : alk. paper)
1. Leadership. 2. Management. 3. Corporate culture. 4. Work environment.
5. Success in business. I. Title.

HD57.7.B3663 2006
658.4′092—dc22   2005022049

ISBN-13: 978-0-87389-669-6
ISBN-10: 0-87389-669-6

Publisher: William A. Tony
Acquisitions Editor: Annemieke Hytinen
Project Editor: Paul O'Mara
Production Administrator: Randall Benson

ASQ Mission: The American Society for Quality advances individual,
organizational, and community excellence worldwide through learning, quality
improvement, and knowledge exchange.

Attention Bookstores, Wholesalers, Schools, and Corporations: ASQ Quality Press
books, videotapes, audiotapes, and software are available at quantity discounts
with bulk purchases for business, educational, or instructional use. For
information, please contact ASQ Quality Press at 800-248-1946, or write to ASQ
Quality Press, P.O. Box 3005, Milwaukee, WI 53201-3005.

To place orders or to request a free copy of the ASQ Quality Press Publications
Catalog, including ASQ membership information, call 800-248-1946. Visit our
Web site at www.asq.org or http://qualitypress.asq.org.

♾ Printed on acid-free paper

Quality Press
600 N. Plankinton Avenue
Milwaukee, Wisconsin 53203
Call toll free 800-248-1946
Fax 414-272-1734
www.asq.org
http://qualitypress.asq.org
http://standardsgroup.asq.org
E-mail: authors@asq.org

Contents

Figures and Tables

Preface

This book is intended to help individuals within an organization better understand how their actions can either help create a productive environment, in which people around them can focus their energies on purposeful work, or can contribute to creating a distracting environment where nothing is quite what it seems and people feel the need to tread warily.

While the book is intended to be meaningful to any individual, its main messages increase in importance with the seniority of the individual because of the greater impact on group behavior that actions by senior managers and corporate executives can have.

The reader may gain some insight into what to expect from the book from the story of how it came to be written.

As someone who learned to analyze data on systems in a statistics department, I worked in applied research, industry, and then consulting. Like many who follow such a path, I gradually moved upstream, first helping with operational data, then with operational design, then with organizational direction.

I became fascinated by the fact that some of the organizations I assisted seemed to implement new systems and ways of working with great success, while others foundered. A particularly humbling aspect of this was that the difference between these two cases did not seem to be correlated to the quality of advice or consulting assistance provided by people like me. In fact, some of our best work in a technical sense seemed to have absolutely no impact whatsoever.

What did seem different were the prevailing attitudes within the organizations and the behavior of those in positions of greatest influence. The senior people in the organizations that moved forward with changes seemed to have a quality of deliberateness and directness that those in the stalled organizations did not possess. I was unable to describe this or attribute it to any causal factor.

At the same time I started keeping a scrapbook in which I amassed a diverse range of snippets from newspapers, magazines, books, and client projects that shed some light on different aspects of how individual behavior impacted group behavior, especially those who took responsibility for the outcomes of the group.

At this point the informed reader is likely to be saying, "Why did you not research the subject of leadership? Surely there are ample volumes published on the subject." The short answer is that I had not yet decided that leadership was the right name for the factor I was looking for. One could say that I was trying to shed light on leadership through exploring followership.

I remember with clarity one encounter on the subject. On starting a new project a group of clients and consultants were at lunch in a pancake house in the U.S. Midwest. One of the clients asked a good question: "Looking at all the projects you have undertaken, what is the single most important success factor?" Two of us replied in unison, "Why, leadership, no question about it."

Luckily the food arrived at this point, and the obvious question of "what about leadership?" never got asked. I say luckily because while we could all have given a long answer to that question, that leaders needed to do a whole lot of stuff like creating vision, empowerment of people, structures, and so forth, I think it's fair to say none of us had a concise answer. The fact that I did not have an answer somehow troubled me, but I set it aside because no one else I had yet encountered had a concise answer that satisfactorily explained system behavior either.

About five years ago I was faced with a choice of either throwing out my scrapbook to make much-needed space in my home office or trying to make some sense of what it contained. I recalled the dilemma in the pancake house and determined that as a senior professional who wished to take pride in my work I should attempt to find a satisfying answer. Also, I had reduced my long-distance traveling by joining a Toronto-based firm, Process Design Consultants, and so had freed up a few hours that I could reinvest.

So the process of writing started, analyzing each piece of the puzzle. Once I had extracted some insight from each page of my scrapbook, I started to fit the pieces together. It resembled the act of trying to complete a jigsaw puzzle when you don't have the box lid that shows what the completed picture should look like.

The perspective on leadership that emerged is, as far as I can judge, applicable to all types of organizations, both those that are for-profit and those that are not-for-profit: government, national, international, global. My aim was to write for all these organizations and to maintain a global perspective on the topic. Though my scrapbook contained examples from mostly U.S., U.K., Canadian, and other English-speaking countries, I believe that the insights apply equally to other cultures.

This is one of the reasons that this book is not intended as a "how-to" manual. The style and methods of implementing the leadership model described in this book need to be attuned to the culture of the organization, on the one hand, and to the natural style and strengths of the individual leader, on the other.

In this regard it is sincerely hoped that the model itself is simple enough to guide a leader's quest for clear intentions in any given situation. A leader who starts with clear intentions is, according to the central premise of the book, likely to make the organization more successful than one who is not.

The book is structured in short chapters, each dealing with a specific aspect of leadership, so that the reader can cover a chapter in a 10-minute lunch break or train ride. The entire book could probably be read while taking an intercontinental or cross-continental plane trip. Each chapter ends with a summary that recaps the main points of the chapter, and can serve as a quick reference resource for the reader.

The first three chapters deal with three key questions: Why do organizations need leadership? What does effective leadership consist of? And why is this kind of leadership in short supply (the leadership gap)? The fourth chapter defines a model for leadership for results.

The next three chapters articulate the three classic barriers to performance that damage organizations and that leadership must prevent or mitigate.

The next 11 chapters explain each component of the leadership model in more detail and show how such behavior helps remove the barriers. In addition there are two chapters providing case studies, one of a company turnaround facilitated by leadership behavior and one of leadership and its impact on project implementation.

The final chapter provides the reader with a series of questions to help them identify the most productive area in which to first apply the insights gained from this book.

Acknowledgments

I cannot say enough about the support I have received throughout the writing of this book from the team at Process Design Consultants, especially Larry Chester and Julia Li.

Larry's insights helped me get started on this project in the first place, and his encouragement all through has meant a lot. The manuscript underwent many, many revisions over several years, and without Julia's patience, practical intelligence, positive attitude, and perseverance it would surely have been lost at sea, and the author with it.

I owe an immense debt of gratitude to the many clients who have provided the insights and examples for this book and are the inspiration behind it. They are people, to borrow a phrase from Peter Senge, "who endeavour to live what is herein described."

My thanks to the team at ASQ Quality Press, especially Annemieke Hytinen and Paul O'Mara, for their professionalism and consideration toward a new author. A special thanks to the reviewers who took the time to wade through manuscripts and provide specific practical advice that greatly improved the book.

To the diverse international band of leaders who did me the great personal favor of reviewing my drafts and giving me not only good advice but much-needed encouragement, I say a huge thank you: Kathy Chan, Dave Cox, Davide Drocco, Dan Patterson, Brian Reid, and Kate Swatridge.

To my family and friends who sustained me and believed in me, even when I doubted myself. Especially Adam and Joseph, who have taught me a lot about give-and-take, and the importance of purpose. And Oriana, my north star, whose values have influenced me so much and whose experiences in organizing volunteer groups has given rise to many more insights in this book than she knows.

1

Why Do Organizations Need Leadership?

Leaders care a lot more than they cure, connect a lot more than they control, demonstrate a lot more than they decide. It's time to bring management and leadership back together and down to earth.

Henry Mintzberg

WHAT IS A LEADER? HOW WILL THIS BOOK HELP LEADERS?

It is widely recognized that leadership is a critical factor in enabling any organization to adapt to its environment, through implementing strategy, thereby surviving and thriving. Unfortunately, little specific guidance is available to help leaders understand what they should be doing.

This book is based on research from a diverse range of fields on human behavior, distilled down to reveal three themes in which leadership behavior is vital if strategy is to supplant status quo as the driving force in an organization.

These three themes—Intentions, Influence, and Information and their typical actions—are described and illustrated by examples.

It is intended to be useful to executives responsible for getting their organizations to follow the strategy they have formulated, as well to all managers responsible for implementing strategy and to individuals who wish to maximize their effectiveness in an organizational context.

In particular we endeavor to provide some practical advice for midlevel managers who may seek to apply the points to leadership at their level and to better understand and manage their environment.

They may well have experienced the impact of poor executive leadership and consequently seek to avoid the same mistakes as they move up the corporate ladder.

We set out a framework for leadership based on three interrelated processes, focused on purpose, relationships, and review. By executing these processes, a leader systematically removes the most common barriers to success and at the same time proactively sets up the conditions for success.

REMOVING BARRIERS TO SUCCESS

These barriers to success, as we shall explain later, are conformity, complacency, and competitiveness. Conformity is the biggest barrier to purpose definition, complacency is the biggest barrier to review, and competitiveness is the greatest hurdle to effective relationships.

What Is Arrogant Complacency?

Arrogant complacency occurs when Sick Sigma decision making replaces Six Sigma decision making.

This is how some managers describe it:

- We realized that there was a lot of room for improvement. When we were subjectively judging our performance, we always gave ourselves high marks for our accomplishments. We were also in the habit of using healthcare industry standards as a way to compare ourselves to other facilities—and no surprise, the comparisons were almost always favorable to us. It had been startling when we discovered that 40 percent of U.S. healthcare costs, across the board, were attributable to waste. *Sister Mary Jean Ryan of SSM Healthcare on obstacles to improvement.*

- Customers may want to "quiz" our capability to meet promises. Do we reply with data or continue to give them "bland assurances"? *Manufacturing manager in global company.*

- Anyone with sufficient rank can start a project off. Then it gathers momentum, somehow survives and moves through the process without a thorough review. There are no hurdles, stage gates, or expectations along the way.

Reviews of measurement numbers—very little review against these numbers, and when it is done, people see it as finger pointing—not much learning resulting from it. *Product development manager in consumer products company.*

What Is Passive Conformity?

Passive conformity occurs when herd thinking replaces hard thinking. This is how some managers describe it:

- "When it comes to doing projects that don't make sense, sometimes we push back with reasons and win but often we are just unable to put forward a convincing case. It seems 'baked-in' that we have to go with the flow." *IT manager in a large retail organization.*

- Don't confuse the edge of the rut with the horizon. *Remark to benchmarking team from international forest products company on generating sufficient purpose/vision.*

- Should run with "sure-fire winner" projects and make them happen, not have a bunch of projects that collectively overpromise and underdeliver. There is no such thing as "low-hanging fruit"; every new project takes effort and resources. *Public sector project manager.*

What Is Adversarial Competitiveness?

Adversarial competitiveness occurs when go-ahead-and-take behavior replaces give-and-take behavior. This is how some managers describe it:

- Gulf too wide between plates, cups, and saucers—and lack of "clatter" between them. *Public sector manager's "coded" statement of the major obstacle to improvement in a process, the lack of management alignment.*

- Would you treat your dog this way? *Senior medical researcher at pharmaceutical company on what it felt like working in a misaligned, fragmented system.*

- Groups don't work well together; the advocacy of ideas is not objective, with an obvious favoring of people's own technologies, not really combining strengths. *Consumer product company—product developer.*

- Managers go to a meeting and then come back and say to their staff, "We'll do it this way." They don't seem to realize that we can't just go from A to Z; there is a lot of alphabet in between. *Supervisor at adhesive manufacturing company describing how change usually got implemented.*

SETTING UP THE CONDITIONS FOR SUCCESS

At first glance, few concepts could seem more obscure than "setting up the conditions for success," yet there are a number of roles that have a significant behind-the-scenes component: roles that are well known, such as a movie producer and a stage magician or conjuror.

Why would anyone say that a leader is like a magician?

Because leaders make projects successful without appearing to directly work on them, and magicians make things change without appearing to touch them.

Because like magicians, the crowd cannot see the connection between what they observe the leader doing and the business outcomes achieved. Put in another way, the leader's role is to focus on "high-leverage actions" that produce disproportionate results. As Peter Senge points out (in *The Fifth Discipline*), the problem with identifying high-leverage actions is that they are "nonobvious" to most participants within the system.

One analogy that Senge refers to for high-leverage actions is the trim tab or "rudder on a rudder." The trim tab acts on the huge rudder of a ship or supertanker and helps turn it, which then turns the ship. This tiny rudder is below the waterline and, while everyone who sees a ship at sea knows that it has a rudder, few know that the rudder itself has a rudder. Likewise, the leader plays the role of this rudder within a rudder for the organization.

My researches have shown that this is the "magic" that executive leaders produce, of small changes applied at precisely the right place and time, to turn big organizational ships and keep them headed on the right course.

My contention is that the path that an initiative follows from inception to completion largely determines the quality of its results. This is true regardless of whether it is a movie, a product launch, or an operating cycle of a business firm. The path is characterized by the people who are attracted by the endeavor's purpose to work on it, the working relationships that enable them to add value, and the information and review opportunities that ensure that they can continually adjust the outcomes to achieve the stated purpose.

The right path ensures that returns to stakeholders are maximized and risks are managed at an acceptable level. Effective leadership behavior keeps the initiative on the right path.

LEADERS DON'T GO WITH THE FLOW; THEY CREATE THE FLOW

Individuals in an organization tend to "go with the flow": what hundreds of people are working on must be the right project. What the CEO says is bound to be right. The technology we've used for 10 years must be the only technology to use. Yet if any improvement is to occur, all these things must be questioned in an open-minded way. While everyone accepts this point in principle, in reality everyone hates having basic assumptions challenged. It upsets their comfortable world. It is the leader's role to continually ask these questions and challenge assumptions without causing chaos or undermining people's confidence about their future.

Why continually? Because organizations are subject to the same laws of entropy as the rest of the universe. Left to their own devices, over time they become disordered and the focus of activities drifts away from the intended purposes that represent the desired outcomes for all stakeholders. A leader's role is to ensure that any undertaking has a clear, valid purpose, that appropriate working relationships are established, and that regular evaluations of activity against purpose are followed by course corrections.

In these terms, leadership is about "creating the flow" rather than going with it.

The natural drift in all organizations, especially large ones, is for a go-with-the-flow attitude to set in at all levels: individual, manager, and executive. If this sounds like a harsh condemnation, it should be remembered that the condition applies to the organization as a whole, within which individuals may still be working very hard, wrestling with problems, and chasing opportunities daily. It's just that at the end of any given month or year, the results are a disappointment to most of the stakeholders. Leadership is a process and has measures. To know whether a leader is effective, we need to ask: Are there common purposes, collective decisions, and credible results?

SUMMARY

Leadership is a critical factor in enabling organizations to adapt, survive, and thrive.

- *Leaders* are defined as executives and senior managers who are responsible for getting their organizations to follow the strategy they have formulated, as managers responsible for implementing strategy, and as individuals seeking to maximize the effectiveness of their own efforts within an organizational context.

- Leadership removes barriers to success. The three common barriers are passive conformity, arrogant complacency, and adversarial competitiveness.

- Leaders do not go with the flow; they consciously create the flow using their own behavior. This is an ongoing process.

- Leaders set up the conditions for success. Like a magician they work behind the scenes to prepare things so that all is ready when the curtain goes up.

- Research explored in this book has uncovered three leadership themes: Intentions, Influence, and Information.

2

What Do Effective Leaders Do?

I don't think of leadership as a position. I don't think of leadership as a skill. I think of leadership as a relationship.

Phil Quigley, CEO Pacific Bell

INSIGHTS INTO HOW EXECUTIVE LEADERS "CREATE THE FLOW"

In this chapter I will discuss further two aspects of leadership proposed in the previous chapter, namely that leaders create the flow and that it is achieved through a lot of behind-the-scenes work.

In particular I wish to highlight the activities of successful executive leaders in order to illustrate how leaders do these two things.

The formal component of the executive role is well documented in management literature. As an active member of a senior management team, the executive leader takes key communication and decision-making actions to:

- Link decisions and projects to strategy and allocate resources.

- Evaluate decisions and projects and authorize changes.

- Manage conflicts and changes arising from the decision or project.

But what of the informal part, the behind-the-scenes work? If this indeed creates the flow, it must somehow direct organizational attention, help people connect and collaborate, and then objectively assess progress and correct their course of action. What does this look like?

A classic article by John Kotter gives a clear insight into this. Kotter interviewed and accompanied 15 executives who were rated highly effective by their peers. He found that these executives spend the bulk of their time interacting with people in their network and using a wide range of influencing tactics to get them to respond to their agenda. Most surprisingly:

- Networks are much wider than just bosses or subordinates. Leaders regularly interact with people who may appear to have nothing to do with the leader's own organization.

- Range of topics discussed is extremely wide, in fact involving virtually everything even remotely associated with their organization and its projects.

- Methods used for influencing are similarly broad: joking, discussing items unrelated to work like family and hobbies, asking a lot of questions and making suggestions, but rarely giving directions (orders) in the traditional sense.

- Interactions are numerous but often of short duration, are disjointed conversations, and are highly opportunistic in the sense that the leader responds to whatever issue the individual raises rather than focusing solely on the executive's own issues.

Kotter characterized this informal way of working as "personal chats with people outside their formal chain of command." His conclusion was that this style of working, which on the surface may seem unproductive, is in fact highly productive. "A chance hallway conversation with a member of their network that lasts two minutes can accomplish as much, if not more, than a formal meeting lasting 30 minutes." How can this be? Because they are not attempting to get decisions made, but instead they are attempting to influence thinking and be influenced by firsthand information and trusted viewpoints. But there is a catch.

Not all impromptu conversations are productive. Some are just random interactions. Kotter concludes that "impromptu conversations are productive only when the agenda is clearly in mind and the network relationships are firmly in place."

The outcome of a leader's impromptu interactions is twofold. On one hand they gain a renewed relationship and on the other they have the opportunity to make suggestions and persuade. They may, if the situation is favorable, just come right out and ask someone to act in a way that supports the agenda. This could involve asking that person to approach another individual in his or her network (but outside the leader's network) with a similar end in mind. The leader may also offer assistance to the individual by offering a trade that may enable a solution or by hosting a meeting where a group-level exchange of intentions and information can take place. In this way the leader's influence in key areas is leveraged to include a large number of people very rapidly.

We have seen how Kotter's research on executive leadership offers some insights into the behind-the-scenes work of leadership, consisting of a series of astute, opportunistic interactions with a wide range of people.

If this does not sound like someone who is not going with the flow, consider that a wise leader knows better than to stand in front of a tide of people and hold up a hand saying "stop." The leader is likely to be swept off his or her feet. A wise leader seeks instead to channel the energies of the organization, not to halt its momentum. This is best done in subtle ways, using the natural behavior of individuals and groups to do the work.

A well-known student prank illustrates such behavior. The student stands in a pedestrian thoroughfare and stares intently up at the top of a building. Soon curious people stop and they too stare upward, trying to locate the source of the fascination. The harder they look, the more it attracts others to stop and join. Soon the sidewalk is filled with upturned faces.

The prankster, well satisfied, now walks off, leaving the crowd to puzzle. Now while it is sincerely hoped that a leader has something much more substantive to do than trick people into staring at nothing, the leader must capitalize on this behavior and ensure that positive behaviors spread instead of negative ones.

LEADERSHIP MODEL

At this point I want to introduce in a little more detail the leadership model arising from the research summarized in this book. As mentioned earlier, this model has three themes: intention, influence, and information.

A somewhat similar model is Garvin's managerial framework, which consists of three processes: direction setting, which sets organizational direction and goals; negotiation and selling, which obtains support and resources; and monitoring and control, which tracks ongoing activities and performance.

We believe this model underpins many of the best leadership and change lessons found in books and articles. As an example, an article by Arthur Fornari and George Maszle of Xerox's lean-Six Sigma initiative explained the leadership challenge that faces the company's Six Sigma deployment.

They listed five key points, of which one was concerned with intentions (project selection linked to business strategies), one was concerned with information (ability to track results using a robust project tracking system), and two were concerned with influence (ability to achieve integration into the business and engage the full value chain in all geographies and operations).

The fifth point dealt with the issue of getting leaders to play the role required in order to address the four other key areas, which they described as "ability to change culture and leadership behavior."

This confirms for us both the central role of leadership behavior and the areas where leaders must become more active and more effective.

In surveying business organizations and industries to find examples of executive leadership, we have found no clearer example than the role of a movie producer within the movie industry.

The cochairmen of Working Title production company, Eric Fellner and Tim Bevan, provide a rare glimpse into how movie production works. Movie production, as described by Fellner and Bevan, is the very essence of leadership.

We believe that leadership consists of three themes, as shown by Figure 2.1.

Figure 2.1 Example of movie producer as leader.

While Working Title have not had a lot of true blockbuster (over $100 million U.S.) movies, it has enjoyed a steady stream of successful movies, such as *Four Weddings and a Funeral, Notting Hill, Elizabeth, Billy Elliot, Fargo, Bridget Jones's Diary, About a Boy, Love Actually,* and *Shaun of the Dead.*

The leverage of film producers can be gauged from the fact that although an average movie crew may number 150 to 200 people, Working Title manages four movies at a time with a staff of 40 people from its low-key offices in London's West End.

LEADER'S RECIPE FOR A GOOD MOVIE: RIGHT SCRIPT, RIGHT CAST, AND RIGHT SCENES

The secret to producing a successful movie, according to Fellner and Bevan, is to start with the right script. As they explain:

"Everyone thinks the big moment is when a film starts shooting, but if you get the script right then you can get the cast right, you get the right people to produce it and shooting is (then) just a process."

In other words, a script is the producer's key tool for selling the purpose behind the movie to actors, to directors, and to financial backers. It is on the basis of the script that contracts are made.

The script is a good metaphor for leadership "intentions" in general. Fellner and Bevan maintain an enviable track record in a highly competitive industry by paying a lot of attention to getting the intention right.

Having clear intentions that all stakeholders can understand removes a lot of an organization's risk from any undertaking.

Fellner and Bevan use the script as a management tool. If the script is not of high quality, they do not proceed. If it is good, they use it to recruit a suitable crew and cast and, most importantly, get financial backers, who will be looking at the potential returns from audiences likely to be interested in that type of movie. The quality of creative writing can be assessed, as Robert Pirsig describes in his classic book, *Zen and the Art of Motorcycle Maintenance.* As an English professor, Pirsig got his class to achieve consensus on what was good-quality writing by discussing their assignments as a group, although they were unable to completely define what made a piece of writing good.

But surely, you say, doesn't every movie producer operate this way? It appears not. Each producer has a personal philosophy for picking and making movies. At one extreme, avant-garde directors may act as their own producer and work without a script at all. At the other end, a producer and a studio may start with a plot idea, a central character, and a large special effects budget, and work backward to create a script.

Fellner and Bevan clearly recognize the importance of "influence." Without building the right relationships, a producer cannot hope to get the buy-in and backing of the Hollywood gatekeepers: the studios, the talent agencies, and the distributors. Nor can a producer count on the later commitment of actors, cast members, and film crews needed to make the movie to high standards and within budget. Fellner and Bevan say that the essence of these negotiations is brinkmanship.

Like many leaders of big projects, Fellner and Bevan often find such negotiations hang in the balance: Will people support it or not? (If they do, it will fly; if they don't, it won't, but don't let them know that.)

"The whole thing is about brinkmanship. It's brinkmanship to get a movie on, it's brinkmanship to get an actor into your movie." In other words, they put a movie project together a piece at a time, through negotiating with many individuals and organizations.

Fellner and Bevan's credibility is sufficiently high with Hollywood that they can give the "green light" for the $25 million that it takes to make a movie without consulting their Hollywood backers. Credibility is a vital leadership tool, and successful influencing cannot be done without it.

The producers don't like to be too involved in the movie production because, as they point out, it's "just a process," and with average film costs of $250,000 per day, any interference at that stage is costly.

They do, however, get heavily involved in evaluating the footage before the movie's release. It is at this point that nearly all of the production costs have been spent, but the budget for marketing and distribution, which cost as much again as production, has not yet been spent.

"You get very, very involved in the editing process because that's the point where it either all comes together, or it doesn't," they say. This is the information theme, reviewing what has worked and what has not. Leaders keep what's working and use it to create an outcome, minimizing or eliminating what's not working.

Movie producers, like good leaders everywhere, make sure that they get personally involved in driving key decisions that have the biggest dollar payback:

- Choosing the right script ideas to make into movies

- Getting the right resources to make the movie on the right terms

- Ensuring that the final footage is right before the movie is released

As a footnote that validates the effectiveness of the "producer" model of leadership, especially in fragmented environments with multiple stakeholders, Sony Corporation announced the appointment in March 2005 of its first non-Japanese CEO, Howard Stringer.

Mr. Stringer's strengths, it was reported, are his ability to create consensus and get tough decisions made. His background? He started off as a TV producer; as he told journalists, "Once a producer, always a producer."

SUMMARY

Effective leaders do a lot of behind-the-scenes work to "create the flow."

- They realize that formal communication and decision making are not enough. Effectiveness comes from numerous networking interactions of short duration that cover multiple topics in many formats, but all supporting a well-thought-out agenda.

- Successful movie producers demonstrate the validity of this model. Starting with clear intentions in the form of a good script, they influence a whole network of backers, agencies, and actors to get behind the project; finally, they review information, by editing the scenes, to create a movie that "works." They stay out of the "operational" aspect of the movie, the actual shooting. Once they have put the right people in charge, their involvement can only be interference.

3

Effective Leaders Are All Too Rare, But They Are Out There

Once we take responsibility for seeing not only from the neck up, but also with the heart, we start to view political correctness and workplace power plays for what they usually are: a sham.

Robert Kooper and Ayman Sawaf
Executive EQ

LEADERS STRETCH PEOPLE'S THINKING WHERE IT MATTERS MOST

What I am describing about leadership are fundamental behaviors that influence a large system.

Earlier I alluded to the fact that in order to channel behavior and "create the flow," leaders need to pick their moments and choose tactics wisely in order to harness human group dynamics. Another way of looking at this is to say leadership behavior co-exists with the culture of the organization (so as not to be rejected like transplanted body tissue) while at the same time "stretching" the culture in critical areas. Behavior in these areas leads to failure if it is driven by fear but to success if driven by fact and faith.

In essence this stretching is to change employees' perception of personal risk and reward to correspond better with the organization's risk and reward.

It is not merely enough for the people to act in a way that is not fear-driven in order to break the spell. They must go further, acting in a way that is driven by fact and faith.

The situation was articulated with chilling clarity by Simone Weil in 1939, as country after country capitulated to the Nazis and collaborated with the new "authorities."

Anyone who is merely incapable of being as brutal, as violent and as inhuman as someone else but who does not practice the opposite virtues is inferior to that person in both inner strength and prestige and will not hold out in a confrontation.

Unfortunately, this calls for a set of competencies that are not easy to develop and that do not develop as a by-product of managing operational tasks.

In fact, the development of these competencies may very well be inhibited by the organization's culture, focused as it often is on those attributes most prized in the conduct of the core activity itself. For example, in a large retailing organization the culture may value and encourage neatness, mastery of detail, quick reactions, attention to customers, and an ability to be "present," or focused on the here-and-now of available product and customers' buying signals. Someone with those skills and attributes may well rise in the management ranks in part because he or she exemplifies what the culture prizes.

Such individuals, taking cues exclusively from those around them, may not be aware that they need to develop a different aspect of themselves in order to fulfill the more senior roles. In addition, they need a personal motivation to "do the job right," above what those around them are asking them for. Unless they have such a drive, they are likely to fall in and "go with the flow" in all cases. Why should they resist?

THE LEADERSHIP GAP

One of the largely unnoticed outcomes of our rapidly changing markets and organizations is that people are propelled upward toward the executive boardroom without any real preparation for the role their organization needs them to play.

A colleague, Larry Chester, with many years' experience in developing managerial skills, puts this problem in perspective with a diagram (Figure 3.1) that shows the (necessarily oversimplified) path of a typical individual progressing from contributor roles through management roles to senior management/executive roles.

These individuals spend time in each role and gradually acquire their skills. The organization, happy with their performance and perhaps seeing potential, promotes them to positions of greater responsibility that call for additional skills, some of which they may not yet possess.

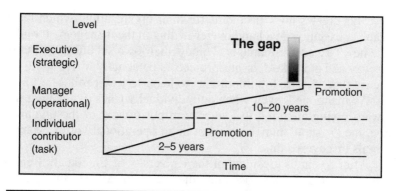

Figure 3.1   Management transitions: The leadership gap.

So they must catch up and close the gap in expectations. Although there are in practice many such steps, the two biggest are going from an individual contributor role to a supervisor/management role and later going from manager to what North Americans refer to as executive roles (direct reports to the head of the organizations) and Europeans may refer to as senior management. Conceptually these steps are similar for the individual: they are drastic changes, and yet organizationally they are very different. In the first case there are many sources of help and examples to learn from; in the second case there are few such sources.

In the early part of their career there are plenty of development opportunities for skills and experience. There are also lots of others who are in the same position, with whom they can compare notes and learn from. In their early promotions they make a shift from doing tasks to managing people who do those tasks. However, there are numerous training courses, books, seminars, and, most importantly, often a number of more senior managers to learn from. There is much to learn and much to cope with, and the issues come thick and fast right from the first day.

Over the years individuals develop skills that enable them to cope fairly effectively with a stream of issues that arise from employees, customers, and other stakeholders. Having demonstrated an ability to cope with operational complexity, the individual is now (if lucky enough) catapulted into the executive ranks.

This is a much bigger jump. For while management positions at least bear some resemblance to the organization's core tasks, like project work or interacting with customers, executive work does not. It is little wonder that many people in reaching the corner office seem to operate exactly as they did when they were managers.

This creates huge problems for their organization, which has a "gap" at executive level and overcrowding in the management ranks. The new "executive-managers" elbow their own subordinates out of the way and grab "key" issues/projects to personally "drive" with the excuse that "they're too important" to leave to lesser folk.

As mentioned, even when an individual wishes to change roles toward giving attention to longer-term positioning of the organization, the "system" may keep them in an operational vortex. Warren Bennis discovered this.

After a year as president of the University of Cincinnati, Bennis discovered that he had become "the victim of a vast, amorphous, unwitting, unconscious conspiracy to prevent me from doing anything whatever to change the University's status quo." Instead of being a leader with an entrepreneurial vision and time to spend thinking about the forces that would affect the destiny of his university, he was mired in issues.

While I was discussing this diagram one day with a family friend who has held executive positions in a number of international corporations, he became quite agitated. The picture, he stated, was often much worse than I was painting it, mainly because these factors all reinforced one another.

For instance, the presence in the executive suite of "super-managers" with strong survival instincts leads to their acting more like roadblocks to leadership development than enablers of it. Also, people in junior management positions believe that they have many years to prepare themselves for senior roles that require leadership skills (whatever they believe them to be) and focus exclusively on the type of specific controlling actions that are expected by their boss and employees in general.

Meanwhile, any natural talents, creativity, or leadership insights they may have glimpsed in themselves as school sports captains or volunteer charitable organizers fall into disuse, and the feelings associated with them fade into memory. As a result, said the retired executive, he had seen many people who had much promise of being effective leaders when young finally arrive at the top floor blunted and worn down. They were thoroughly accustomed to going with the flow.

In such an environment, middle managers who occasionally wonder whether they should be providing more leadership (perhaps reading what is written on the faces of their team) can quickly convince themselves that such actions would only be called for in the event that they themselves saw leadership behavior in their boss. This, said my friend, is no excuse. Because of the interconnectedness of the organization, genuine leadership at any level has significant influence. In the short term it changes what is possible for their teammates and colleagues, and in the long term it changes what is possible for the organization.

In this regard I was reminded of W. Edwards Deming's story about a small research project he assisted with at New York University's Graduate School of Business. The university set out to discover whether any of its teachers had made a lasting impact on its students. By surveying past students, the university discovered that six names were prominent, and these names came as a complete surprise as they had received no particular awards or distinctions while at the university. No one had recognized their efforts at the time.

Many of the examples in this book are examples of this type of entirely self-motivated leadership. Providing leadership was for these people part of doing the job right, and it was not done to increase their chances of promotion or to receive a commendation, bonus, or vote of thanks.

Fortunately many organizations are waking up to the bottom-line impact of effective leadership and are devoting appropriate resources and focus to encourage and develop leadership behavior throughout their organization. In a world of global markets, rapid technology transfer, ready access to capital, and wafer-thin profit margins, many companies are searching for a source of advantage that is hard to duplicate. Consequently a new generation of corporate leaders is going beyond lip service in pursuit of both practicing and preaching the message of effective leadership.

For example, exceptional results by PepsiCo (*Business Week,* January 10, 2005) in growing its key international markets have been attributed directly by its CEO, Steve Reinemund, to its investment in developing leaders in each of those markets, who made it happen at the local level.

What competencies need to be developed in order to be a successful leader?

COMPETENCIES THAT LEADERS NEED

From John Kotter's interviews and observations emerged a set of requirements for the development of leaders. In order to be in a position to conduct their influence campaigns effectively and create alignment, Kotter argues, leaders must know the business, the organization, and its people well and have the following skills:

- Engage in long-range strategic thinking to identify both objectives and initiatives for accomplishing them. Seek out ideas, proposals, programs, and projects that can help accomplish multiple objectives. This is the key competency for the Intentions theme and will be discussed in detail in later chapters.

- Engage in network relationship building using an invaluable ability to relate to people as individuals. This is the key competency for the Influence theme and will be discussed in detail in later chapters.

- Aggressively seek information on what's really happening (including bad news) and assimilate it. Skillfully ask questions and listen attentively to the answers. This is the key competency for the Information theme and will be discussed in more detail in later chapters.

These competencies are sometimes described using different language, as a quick review of some recent job advertisings shows.

Many organizations recognize the need for their senior people to have a clear sense of purpose. The "intention dimension" is a common requirement for the most senior role.

This is emphasized in print more often by public service or not-for-profit organizations than by business organizations. For example, two institutes, one in Europe and one in South America, that recently advertised for directors both sought a person with clear intentions that could inspire their organizations.

The natural history museum in London sought candidates who "demonstrate their leadership by expressing a clear personal vision that delivers excellence in all the museum's activities."

The International Potato Center in Lima, Peru, wanted someone with "a clear vision of the way science and technology can contribute to improving the livelihoods of the poor."

The relationship-building role of senior level people is usually framed as "motivation" of employees. Relationship building is referred to in the context of external stakeholders only. Thus the Influence dimension is generally present in requirements for senior jobs but is described in vague and often inconsistent terms.

The United Kingdom's forestry commission, responsible for overseeing the sustainable management of Britain's forests, in its search for a director general stipulated that the successful candidate must have "a natural flair for persuasion and for building productive relationships."

The Information dimension is the least mentioned of the three in senior job requirements, perhaps because it is considered such a commonplace skill set and attitude that it is not worth mentioning. As I intend to show in the remainder of this book, the truth is very far from this.

Some organizations do see the need for leaders who can evaluate a situation and take action, although the need for such changes is phrased in positive terms and the role of fact-based decisions is totally overlooked.

For instance, the University of Luton's advertising for a chief executive stated that "there is much achievement on which to build but challenges lie ahead and major initiatives wait to be taken." Likewise, an independent charitable healthcare foundation, the King's Fund, sought a chief executive who needed to "reposition the King's Fund within its current assets, whilst developing a strategy to identify new income generating opportunities."

SUMMARY

Many organizations do not encourage people to develop their leadership skills.

- Leadership behavior is not expected until people reach the executive suite. By the time most employees get there, they are not motivated to change and are stuck with being control-oriented managers.

- Despite wordy statements in training manuals, many organizations discourage the practice of effective leadership because it requires a tolerance of questioning and a deeper sense of loyalty to stakeholders than to any particular pet project, company initiative, or highly placed individual.

- This results in a leadership gap at the top of many organizations, leaving them rigid, brittle, and at the mercy of major changes to their environment.

- In spite of this, many people try to provide effective leadership to their teams or organizations because they are driven to do the job right according to their own standards. This has a significant impact, although it may not be recognized or rewarded at the time.

- The three themes of Intentions, Influence, and Information correspond well with research by Kotter on competencies needed for effective leadership. Organizations advertising senior positions do ask for competencies corresponding to the three themes, although the scope typically described is much narrower than it needs to be.

4

Key Leadership Steps in Each Theme

The zigzag path of an ant on a pebbled beach is due to the complexity of the environment in which the ant is operating, not the complexity of the control strategy in the ant's brain.

Patrick Henry Winston

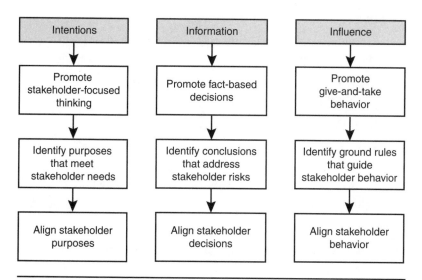

Figure 4.1 Leadership model: Three simultaneous themes.

The leadership model introduced in Chapter 1 has three themes, three prominent and recurring topics or, as musicians would say, melodies.

In this chapter we will introduce further detail about the three themes. Leadership involves three critical interrelated themes, namely Intentions, Influence, and Information. Each of these themes follows a three-step process that involves first gaining involvement from a specific group of people, then creating something that synthesizes their input and embodies their commitments, and finally leveraging these to create alignment.

A leader should make it a priority to allocate time to perform three activities: promote, identify, and align.

The similarity of this structure to the leadership themes is not merely for the sake of simplicity, although that is a strong virtue in matters of behavior, but is because these themes all aim to guide behavior in each of three areas.

Promote, identify, and *align* have communication and demonstration components. The following definitions may help illustrate this logic.

Promote

- Communication: give publicity to something in order to increase awareness.

- Demonstration: attempt to ensure the adoption of something.

Identify

- Communication: recognize, indicate, and distinguish something.

- Demonstration: associate closely with something and build strong links to it.

Align

- Communication: put things in their appropriate relative position.

- Demonstration: give practical support to something, as an ally.

Taking the model for leadership defined earlier, and showing the three-step process for each theme, gives a nine-part model (Figure 4.1).

During the remainder of this book, this model will be explained in more detail, with each chapter dealing with one step within a theme.

It has been often observed that a leader's words and deeds must match if they are to be believed and followed. It is my contention that the more completely and consistently each activity is conducted by a leader, the more successful the leader will be.

This communication and demonstration occurs hour by hour throughout a leader's day. An analysis of the things they have said and done throughout the day will show leaders whether their conduct is helping people focus their stray thoughts and feelings or is scattering them to the four winds. What are the key "somethings" that the leader is promoting, identifying, and aligning? Or are their pronouncements and reactions random and not reflective of the leaders' true beliefs and aspirations for their organization or themselves?

This consistency and completeness is important because activities and behaviors within the three themes do not impact the organization as separate forces but in combination. This multiplies the positive impact of considered and consistent behavior across the three themes. Conversely, it gives discordantly mixed messages when behavior is highly inconsistent.

While effective leaders know it is foolish to attempt to do too many things at once, they build each effective intervention (conversation, decision, meeting, and so forth) like a great stage play or movie with one major storyline and one or more subplots. So at the same time that a leader is promoting give-and-take behavior, he or she may also refer to specific stakeholder needs or the importance of using data to reach decisions on how to serve stakeholders better.

Warren Bennis highlights the greater success of leaders who use a pulling, rather than pushing, style to get employees' commitment. He attributes this to a belief that a pull style of influence attracts and energizes people to enroll in an exciting vision of the future. It motivates through identification rather than through rewards and punishment. In contrast, the push style imposes change rather than inspiring it, which leads only to a more adversarial environment, with people walking around perpetually angry. The pull style, he argues, when used consistently in conjunction with a clearly articulated purpose and vision, can gradually involve all stakeholders in the process of change. Bennis further suggests that the leader who uses the resulting dissent and conflict in a creative and positive way can enable a new set of shared assumptions, a new paradigm, to emerge. This is a lucid description of the leadership theme of influence.

One particular example of this leadership behavior in action was recently published in *Harvard Business Review*. David Garvin and Michael Roberto got permission from a leader to observe what he did over a six-month period in which the leader (Paul Levy of Beth Israel

Deaconess Medical Center, otherwise known as BIMDC Hospital) attempted to turn around performance and create a positive future for his organization.

In our retelling of the story we have organized Garvin and Roberto's account under the headings of the model.

Levy's first phase of action involved promoting key behaviors:

Communication via e-mail to all staff.

- Intentions: promoting stakeholder-focused thinking by urging staff to help save a worthy organization. As Levy wrote, "This is a wonderful institution, representing the very best in academic medicine, exemplary patient care, extraordinary research and fine teaching."

- Information: promoting data-based decision making by urging staff to read the soon-to-be-released independent consultant's report that showed the hospital's desperate financial situation. In Garvin's summary, he writes: "in the absence of a turnaround, the hospital would be sold to a for-profit chain, and would therefore lose its status as a Harvard teaching hospital."

- Influence: promoting give-and-take behavior by letting staff know that they could expect to see him making some difficult decisions, such as "There will be reductions in staff." But he would welcome input and suggestions on the turnaround plan, by e-mail, intranet, or just stopping him in the hallway.

Demonstration of key behaviors.

- Levy responded to 300 staff e-mails, many of which he incorporated into the turnaround plan.

- He conducted many face-to-face hallway conversations with staff to explain his actions and hear input.

Levy's second phase, aimed at identifying the actions needed, was composed of focused communication and reinforcing demonstration.

Communication via cover letter attached to the turnaround plan.

- Intentions: identified, and identified himself with, the hospital's mission, strategy, and values.

- Influence: identified some unpopular actions that were necessary which were needed to implement the plan and that staff had made significant inputs to. (The implied ground rule: I'll take your input into the plan then you can expect that I will implement that plan.)
- Information: identified conclusions about the risks of the plan failing that he anticipated must be on staff's mind. As Garvin wrote, Levy "explicitly diagnosed past plans and explained their deficiencies."

Demonstration.

- Levy drafted guidelines for behavior in key areas such as decision making and conduct of meetings, and he circulated them, discussed them, and stated that everyone, including himself, should be following them. As Garvin stated, "The purpose of these rules was to introduce new standards of interpersonal behavior, and in the process, to combat several dysfunctional routines."
- When a department head publicly flouted these ground rules, Levy took immediate action. Garvin describes how Levy "responded to the same audience publicly denouncing (the individual) . . . for his tone, his lack of courtesy and his failure to speak up earlier in the process, as required by the new meeting rules."

Levy's third phase was aimed at aligning actions and behaviors to get results, and involved communication, again via e-mail to all staff, shortly after a major round of staff layoffs.

Communication.

- Influence: expressing empathy with the natural feelings of sadness that staff felt at the departure of colleagues. This empathy expressed support for staff feelings and helped to keep a perspective on the hospital's values as the ultimate ground rules.
- Intentions: urging staff to maintain focus on their target. "Our target is not just survival; it is to thrive and set an example. A unique academic medical center. . . ."
- Information: a few weeks later a follow-up e-mail, urging alignment with the plan, stating that early signs were favorable but that there was still much work to do to contain costs.

Demonstration.

- When employees asked Levy to intervene as CEO in a
  decision that had been made by departments but not yet
  implemented, he would review it against the guidelines to
  see whether these had been applied. Garvin writes that
  Levy would "review the process used . . . to determine if
  it followed the rules. If so the decision stands."

- When early results showed real improvement, Levy
  reinforced these good efforts, says Garvin. He "convened
  a series of open, question and answer forums, where
  employees heard more details about the hospital's
  tangible progress and received kudos for their
  achievements."

In these first six months Paul Levy led a turnaround in results. In
fact, results for the first year, as reported by Garvin and Roberto,
were better than the turnaround plan called for.

This is a particularly good case to look at from the point of view
that Levy used all-staff e-mail communication as a major tool, allowing the researchers to analyze the content and timing of his communications. And yet we are often told these days by experts in change
management, that e-mail should not be the medium for delivering
key messages; it should always be face to face.

From our viewpoint, the caution about the use of e-mails is no
doubt valid. However, if there is one thing that this model empha-
sizes it is that effective leadership behavior results from a consistent
pattern of actions taken over a period of time. Leadership actions can
rarely be understood from a single event. Paul Levy was in an
unusual position: he was an "outsider," did not know the managers in
the organization, could not wait for them to get in line with his plan,
and, in fact, may have believed them to be part of the problem. So he
decided to communicate directly to staff and, crucially, his communications were matched closely by his actions.

The lesson of this case is that a broadcast message is only as
good as the actions that follow it. As people came to realize that the
communications accurately described what was going to happen,
they no doubt started reading them more closely. If, as is very likely,
there were a number of people who ignored the first e-mail, their
work colleagues would soon have informed them of what its key
points were, and when subsequent events turned out as described,
they would take more care to study future e-mails from Levy.

After all, Winston Churchill could not visit every British house-
hold, nor tour occupied Europe in World War II, but he still managed

to get people to follow his lead by acting decisively in complete accordance with the messages given in his radio broadcasts.

Another key point is that every organization is different. If someone were to attempt exactly the same steps as Levy in exactly the same way for another organization, it might not work. Levy himself credits a key part of the turnaround to the staff's incredibly high sense of dedication to their hospital and the work it did for the community. Levy tapped into this and with good planning and effective leadership behavior created a turnaround situation.

In concluding my overview of the leadership model, I am aware that I have created many questions in the reader's mind that remain unanswered. The subsequent chapters of the book are intended to answer those questions. In the next chapter, I will revisit the question of why these themes are important. The next three chapters will describe what I believe are the three main contagious viruses that infect organizational thinking and cripple constructive action. The themes will then be positioned as antidotes to these conditions in the chapters that follow.

Each of the three steps within each theme will then be described and illustrated in its own chapter.

The final chapter brings together a summary of the key lessons of the model and provides questions to help the readers assess how best to implement this model and learn from it in their own environment.

SUMMARY

The leadership model is explained in more detail, with three steps of promote, identify, and align within each of the three themes.

- Each step within each of three themes has both a communication and a demonstration component. This "say" and "do" must be consistent in order for full impact to be gained.

- The more steps that are strung together in a sequence according to the model, the greater the impact these actions will have, as each consistent communication and action builds upon the last, with increasing power and resources.

- In a case study involving a teaching hospital, the leader's actions in turning around performance can be seen as using the Intentions, Influence, and Information themes within each phase of his plan.

5

Barrier #1: Passive Conformity

The unfortunate truth is that most of the time people who come forward and speak up are dishonored.
Dennis Arter and J. P. Russell, "Ethics, Auditing and Enron," *Quality Progress,* October 2003

CONFORMITY AND WHY IT'S A PROBLEM

Passive conformity occurs when people in an organization abdicate entirely their responsibility to think about the future and leave it to others, often their boss.

It is generally accepted in any organization or community that certain individuals have greater experience of specific matters and should be listened to more than others. In addition, certain people may have been given responsibility and authority to make specific decisions on behalf of others.

However, blind obedience, or unquestioning obedience to those in authority, is an unhealthy behavior for the organization and for the success of those in authority. No one can know everything, be everywhere, or see everything. Nor can any one individual look out for all the needs of all individuals in the organization, both short term and long term. Ultimately all individuals need to take some responsibility for their own welfare.

Unquestioning obedience is one form of going with the flow. One principle that expresses this behavior is "where the chief sits is the head of the table."

A stark example of what can happen when those in authority are obeyed without question occurred in 1893. The British Navy this time provides the lesson. An admiral was on maneuvers with his flotilla of battleships. From his flagship he gave an order: "Form the fleet into columns of two divisions, six cables apart, and then reverse the course by turning inwards."

At face value this sounds dangerous, telling ships to get into parallel lines and then turn toward each other.

His second in command however, keen to prove his obedience, failed to seriously question (or clarify) these orders but passed them on verbatim. Alas, as every sailor could see, the combined turning circles of the ships was greater than the distance in between them and two ships collided. One, HMS *Victoria,* sank.

Should the naval officers have disobeyed the order? Not outright, perhaps, but there are many ways that they could have clarified the situation and given the admiral an opportunity to provide more clear instruction or reconsider his order.

Such situations have been found to be a major contributory cause of serious incidents in the armed forces in which people were accidentally fired on and innocent lives were lost. Inquires into such tragedies inevitably reveal that those in command had not built relationships in which their subordinates felt their opinions were valued. So when the pressure was on and a bad order was given, people just stood by as the disaster unfolded, offering no helpful input that could have avoided the mistake.

All of that underlines the importance of leaders being able to acquire enough valid information to make sound decisions.

This is illustrated by tragedies at the National Aeronautics and Space Administration (NASA).

CORROSIVE CONFORMITY AT NASA

Even NASA, which provides positive examples from the Apollo flights (later in this book), has seemingly lost its way in recent years. As the investigation into the tragedy of the space shuttles Columbia and Challenger revealed, NASA's management culture hampered effective decision making in ways similar to those outlined in this chapter.

At 6:59 A.M. on February 1, 2003, the Columbia broke apart as it reentered the atmosphere. All seven crew members perished. The subsequent investigation established that a 1.67-pound slab of supercooled insulating foam had broken off from the external tank and punched a hole in the leading edge of the left wing of Columbia 81.7 seconds after its launch two weeks earlier.

The investigation also established that bureaucratic conditions in NASA, allowing the foam incident to occur in the first place and then allowing its implications to go undetected during the mission, were just as important as the strike itself. As the foam incident with the shuttle Discovery showed, these problems were unfortunately still not resolved in 2005.

In a scathing 248-page report on Columbia, a team of 13 investigators concluded the beleaguered space agency, battling a steadily declining budget, had learned little from the 1986 Challenger explosion, which also killed seven astronauts, and that a sense of infallibility permeated its decision making. For example, a late-hour rescue mission using the shuttle Atlantis, while risky, might have been possible, the investigators said. NASA officials never gave the option a chance.

Reports confirmed that NASA's structure and culture made decision making very difficult. For example, requests to view satellite images of the shuttle after launch to assess damage became lost in the system.

In any endeavor, our purpose guides our actions to make sure we carry out the right actions. This understanding of what we are trying to accomplish is invaluable when choices have to be made. Our task becomes selecting the option that best achieves our purpose.

BOSSES SET THE TONE ON HOW MUCH CONFORMITY THEY EXPECT

But herein lies a paradox about purpose. It is clear instinctively that the most senior and powerful individuals define the purpose. In an enlightened organization/company, the senior person will take into account the needs and aspirations of all stakeholders. But in an unenlightened (or authoritarian) community, the senior person will tend to reflect only his or her own needs.

The paradox is that if the purpose is not clear to us or is invalid (it appears to not meet anyone's needs), we know that we should "ask the chief to clarify it." Unfortunately this is typically the last person we wish to question. If they volunteer the information, all is well, but if they do not want to? Whose job is it to query the purpose? Why should any of us take the risk of offending the chief?

Consequently, purpose tends to be questioned least in the organizations that need it most.

A famous Scottish warrior, Rob Roy MacGreggor, coined a saying that sums up this situation well: "Where MacGreggor sits is the head of the table." In other words, whatever the chief says is our purpose.

At the heart of conformity is what we might call the "emperor has no clothes" syndrome. Fear and anxiety work their way subtly through the organization to cause a silence where there should be forthright information given and considered opinions offered. In the children's story, an emperor is persuaded by an ingenious con man to buy a nonexistent suit of clothes and his subjects are too scared to tell him that when he dresses in this "suit" he is, in fact, naked. Finally, he encounters a child who, knowing no better, tells him the naked truth.

Author Sydney Finkelstein, in his book *Why Smart Executives Fail, and What You Can Learn from Their Mistakes,* argues that studying excellence alone offers an unbalanced picture of corporate life. There is considerable value, he argues, in studying failure in a systematic way.

One striking conclusion that Finkelstein reaches is that these executives all insisted on absolute unquestioning obedience, or conformity, from their followers. The symptoms of this were threefold. First, personalization: they identify so completely with the organization that there is no clear boundary in their mind between their personal interests and organizational interests. The organization is an extension of their ego. Second, overconfidence: they seem to have all the answers, often dazzling people with the speed and decisiveness with which they deal with challenging matters. Third, a policy of no dissention: they make sure everyone is 100 percent behind them, ruthlessly eliminating anyone who they suspect might undermine their efforts.

HOW HERD THINKING REPLACES HARD THINKING

An individual or organization that adopts the practice of hard thinking focuses on the needs of their stakeholders and then figures out what to do. Conversely an individual or organization that adopts the practice of herd thinking figures out what they think by focusing on what those around them seem to be doing. But how does such behavior propagate through a large organization and inhibit so many people?

The roots of this behavior lie in authoritarian tendencies, meaning a willingness to conform uncritically to standards and commands that are supported by authority figures. Psychologists tell us that this is usually related to ego deficiencies.

It is my belief that all organizations are vulnerable to the growth of authoritarian tendencies, the seeds of which seem to be everpresent and ready to sprout and spread like weeds in a garden. Such tendencies are particularly insidious in light of the fact that many people in the organization, when they cooperate with an authoritarian cultural tendency, are acting contrary to their personal beliefs and values. Worse still, by swelling the ranks of its supporters they are unwittingly helping coerce their colleagues into participating.

Do not confuse authoritarian behavior with similar-sounding terms like *authoritative* or *autocratic*. Just like a humanitarian is someone who is motivated by a love of people and humanity, an authoritarian is someone who is motivated by a love of power and those in power. This tendency is destructive in all but the smallest doses.

Conversely, those who are authoritative (powerful) or autocratic (wielding solo power) can definitely serve their organizations well in the appropriate circumstances.

One of the most compelling explanations of creeping authoritarian behavior is by Karl Weick:

> On the basis of avoided tests, people conclude that constraints exist in the environment and that limits exist in their repertoire of responses. Inaction is justified by implantation; in fantasy, of constraints and barriers that make action "impossible." These constraints, barriers and prohibitions then become prominent "things" in the environment. They also become self-imposed restrictions on the options that (people) consider and exercise when confronted with problems (and decisions).

In other words, we put up barriers in our mind and every time we consciously avoid them it strengthens our belief that they exist.

If an organization or project does not have a clear purpose defined, the structure and resources will not be lined up against a clear purpose but will reflect a fragmented purpose. The stakeholders who are in a position to influence these elements will have seen to it that only their own requirements are reflected. In these circumstances there is zero chance that the unrepresented aspects of purpose would be fulfilled by accident.

Often this omission is spotted later in the organization's life cycle, when it is hard to correct. Now organizational groups are entrenched and have invested resources and reputations along specific lines. Consequently, resistance to efforts to define purpose will be fierce. "You're trying to change the rules!" will be the cry. Those seeking such a course will find themselves accused of self-serving motives. In most cases the resistance is insurmountable unless external stakeholders put significant pressure on the system. This creates a near crisis, which the CEO (business or unit head) can use as an opportunity to refocus the organization around a new purpose.

GROUP-THINK AND CONFORMITY

When we mention herd thinking, the phrase that often jumps into people's minds is *group-think,* a phenomenon first described by I. L. Janis. He researched four of the United States' worst military/ political setbacks and identified the crucial role played in each case by committees of otherwise competent, conscientious individuals who seemingly abandoned rational thinking while members of an advisory group to the commander or commander in chief. Janis gives six causal factors that he believes were at work within those groups. They seem to me to have a potent mixture of both passive conformity (stereotyping, shared illusions, silence means consent) and arrogant complacency (felt invulnerability, unquestioning, ignoring of information), as befits really disastrous outcomes.

The best known of Janis's case examples, the Bay of Pigs fiasco, became a byword for disastrously flawed thinking. The newly elected president, John Kennedy, was advised to give the go-ahead to an invasion of Cuba by CIA-trained Cuban exiles. The plan was based on six crucial assumptions, each of which turned out to be utterly false; worse still, they could easily have been discovered ahead of time to be false had any efforts been made to check them.

A rueful Kennedy remarked, "How could I have been so stupid as to let them go ahead?" This author believes, without any solid evidence, that Kennedy learned important lessons about using advisors. He later put those lessons to good use in his skillful handling of a nuclear standoff with the Soviet Union known as the Cuban missile crisis.

SUMMARY

Passive conformity is a major barrier to productive work and one that leadership action must combat.

- Conformity occurs where people abdicate their responsibility to think about the future. The people at the top of the organization set the tone on how much conformity they expect.

- Conformity means that herd thinking replaces hard thinking.

- Conformity spreads and strengthens its hold as imagined limitations are reinforced by the community.

- In cultures in which high conformity has evolved, there tends to be a marked deference to positions and rank. People are extremely reluctant to question assumptions or think for themselves at work, without express permission. Pronouncements of organizational leaders are accepted at face value and a variety of unrelated actions are undertaken in their name, without any real understanding of what they are trying to do, what has been done, or what should happen next. What the boss says is automatically taken as the official and last word on any subject; "Where the chief sits is the head of the table."

- Passive conformity is a major barrier to communicating clear intentions, because the culture assumes that intentions are whatever the boss or other powerful stakeholder have implied they should be.

6

Barrier #2: Adversarial Competitiveness

Environments are invisible. Their ground rules, pervasive structure and overall patterns elude easy perception.

Marshall McLuhan

ADVERSARIAL COMPETITIVENESS AND WHY IT'S BAD NEWS

Another type of going-with-the-flow behavior is to treat everyone we encounter as a rival to be competed with, to be bested.

The saying "never give a sucker an even break" is attributed to the American comedic actor W. C. Fields, whose stage persona was that of an irascible, world-weary wheeler-dealer, almost a confidence trickster. His logic was that people who didn't know what they were doing (suckers) were destined to be duped and by treating them fairly you were breaking nature's laws and would surely be punished. To Fields's character, people who were dumb enough to be deceived were not smart enough to appreciate that you had treated them fairly and were just as likely to complain as when you cheated them! Furthermore, the next operator on the scene would surely do what you failed to do and part the suckers from their cash. In fact, suckers may be taken in to a greater extent the second time because their view that they are smart has been reinforced by your foolishly benign treatment of them. So, in a nutshell, both they and you will be worse off if you give them an even break!

Our example takes place in 1850. British and French forces were at war with Russia, in the Crimean War. British forces had suffered huge losses, mainly because they lacked basic military goods such as food, fuel, and shelter. One particular action was destined to become legendary, immortalized by the poet Tennyson in "The Charge of the Light Brigade." The poem describes vividly the courage of cavalrymen in riding up a valley flanked by cannons and attacking the Russian front line, an action in which they suffered 85 percent casualties. All this tragedy was caused by a misunderstanding magnified by a chain of communication dominated by competitiveness and intense personal dislike.

The supreme commander, Lord Raglan, issued an order that was vague, to say the least. It is written down by his quartermaster-general (Airey) then carried by an aide (Captain Nolan) to the divisional commander (Lord Lucan) and from him to the corps commander (Lord Cardigan). At no point are the instructions clarified by any conversations between the parties. The reason for this is that their personal relationships with each other are dominated by mutual dislike, pride, and jealousy. Ultimately these personal dislikes completely overwhelm their professional conduct.

The final link in the chain of command, Lord Cardigan must have understood the implications of carrying out the order (as communicated to him), because he could see the Russian positions and could imagine only too well what the results would be of attacking them. That he chose not to get clarification from his superior (who was in fact his brother-in-law!), but preferred to send men to certain death, is testimony to the corrosive effects of cultivating such personal dislikes.

How many projects have galloped to destruction because people at senior levels could not or did to wish to talk to each other!

At the heart of this belief is the fear that others will take advantage of us, if we do not first take advantage of them. In this view, cooperation is a remote possibility and a poor strategy. In order to understand the appeal of "never give a sucker an even break," it is necessary to understand the types of decision-making options available to each of two people who are free to choose their negotiating strategy. These options are to compete with the other party or to cooperate. Individuals choose their strategy based on their beliefs and values, in particular what they think the other party will do. In many situations in organizational life, the benefits to both individuals and the organization are greatest when both of them cooperate, but the benefits are still substantial for an individual who competes while the other party cooperates, and they are very small when both parties compete. This situation is known as the "prisoners' dilemma," and its dynamics influence organizational behavior in profound ways. I will quickly review how it plays out.

THE PRISONERS' DILEMMA, OR HOW GO-AND-TAKE BEHAVIOR REPLACES GIVE-AND-TAKE BEHAVIOR

An individual or organization that practices give-and-take behavior seeks to understand the needs of the other party in any situation, and acts to further those needs in addition to their own. Conversely an individual or organization that practices go-and-take behavior seeks to understand how to further their own needs through actions. The prisoner's dilemma can help us understand the linkage between these two modes of behavior.

A man sits in a bare room. There is only a worn table and three old wooden chairs. The man looks worried and looks hesitantly at the two people sitting across the table from him. The two are police officers, and he is a suspect in a criminal investigation. Down the hall in a similar room sits a woman, also a suspect, who is also being questioned. This is a familiar scene in television police dramas.

The woman is also worried. Will he keep quiet and give nothing away, or will he talk? If he blames it all on her and agrees to give evidence against her, he will be rewarded with a light sentence or maybe none at all. On the other hand, if they both say nothing incriminating, they know the police will find it almost impossible to make their case. But, she asks herself, can I trust him? In his room, the man is wondering whether he can trust her.

Faced with the uncertainty of each partner's trustworthiness and the certainty of a severe punishment if their partner does talk, each individual will almost inevitably take the opportunity to sell out their confederate. This happens in spite of the fact that each knows that if they stick together they will both come out well.

At the heart of the prisoners' dilemma is the notion that this is a one-time situation and we will never encounter the other player again, and if we do they will not be in a position to hurt us by taking revenge or even by rebuking us publicly.

The reason that the prisoners' dilemma is such an effective model for many of our relationships is that so many of our dealings with others are as an anonymous customer or as an arm's-length coworker and the other player has few sanctions; even if they do have some, they have few opportunities to use them.

Aside from moral or ethical considerations, the existence of the prisoners' dilemma inside organizations, between people who should be working together to achieve the organization's purpose, poses a constant danger to the achievement of that purpose. The rules for success used by those who rise in organizations quickly become an established part of the culture, thereby influencing everyone's approach to such situations. In other words, a "look after No. 1" culture can develop from a few instances of people being rewarded after making suckers out of those who cooperated with them.

IMPACT OF COMPETITIVENESS BETWEEN SUPERVISOR AND EMPLOYEE

A story of a university student's summer job illustrates this point well.

Owen Cherrington, a professor at Brigham Young University, once had a vacation job at a food company while he was a student. He had an experience that taught him how prevalent and damaging the "compete" strategy can be in an organization.

Cherrington was hired as an operator in a plant that processed green beans. His supervisor told him to clean up and restart a grading machine every time it jammed. The grader sorted the beans into different sizes. After watching the machine for a while and experimenting, Cherrington found that the jams could be avoided altogether by adjusting the gates to allow equal quantities of beans to flow into each channel. However, this adjustment would only last for while; the vibration of the machine eventually disturbed the settings and they needed readjustment.

He eventually began to see his job as a series of stages. First he spent about an hour adjusting the settings to get the machine running smoothly with equal flow to all channels, then he would watch the machine for signs that a reset was needed. He timed how long the machine went without readjustment and took satisfaction in continually setting "records."

Now remember that his supervisor had originally told him that his job was to fix jams in the machine. This supervisor would occasionally walk by while the machine was operating, and this nearly always corresponded to a time when Cherrington was watching the machine and timing for a record. He did not see the need to discuss with Cherrington how he was doing the job, presumably because he thought he knew much more than the student helper. We can also assume that Cherrington was in no hurry to go to his supervisor voluntarily with this information as a reaction to latter's attitude toward him.

So the supervisor and the manager decided that the machine seemed to be running so smoothly that a full-time operator was no longer needed and that the supervisor could keep an eye on it himself. Luckily, there was an opening in the nearby warehouse that Cherrington could go to; otherwise he could have been let go.

Cherrington had some inkling what was going to happen under the new regime, and so he slipped back to the grading machine on his break from his new job to see what was happening. Watching from the shadows he saw the two managers cleaning up a large pile of beans from the floor, the machine itself jammed. After a few days his previous boss asked him to return to look after the grader. He declined in favor of staying in with the warehouse job, which was more varied. Again, according to Cherrington's account, he did not volunteer any insight into how the machine should be operated to prevent jams, and neither did the supervisor and manager ask him for his advice. He interpreted that as a judgment that they didn't need his help and that they didn't offer him any respect. No doubt they were trying to maintain the belief that a wet-behind-the-ears university student couldn't solve a problem that men with years of experience hadn't solved.

This story gives us a vivid insight into how much waste and loss occurs to individuals and organizations caused by the strategy of "never give a sucker an even break."

HOW A CULTURE OF COMPETITIVENESS TAKES HOLD

Dr. Stephen Covey, in his book *The 7 Habits of Highly Effective People,* identifies a number of key symptoms that, once they become evident to people in the organization, become accepted as a starting point for everyone's dealings.

Let's look first at an individual "winner" mentally. It's someone who refuses to acknowledge the reality of interdependence. It's people who talk win/win but don't want to listen; they want to manipulate. They don't want others to lose; they're just focused on getting what they want, leaving others to take care of their own interests. A second symptom is refusal to face up to relationship difficulties at the top. Competitiveness at the top sets the tone for the rest of the organization. Covey asserts that it takes more nobility of character to confront and resolve issues between executives than it does to continue to diligently work for the many projects and people "out there." The third symptom is the inability to work for common goals. It is an inability to jointly define priorities, an inability or lack of desire to organize around those priorities, and a lack of discipline to execute around them.

In *The Silmarillion*, J. R. R. Tolkien described how this self-sustaining set of beliefs can be quickly spread through a community. "He that sows lies in the end shall not lack of a harvest, and soon he may rest from toil indeed while others reap and sow in his stead. Ever there are ears that will heed and tongues that will enlarge what they hear, and the lies pass from friend to friend, as secrets of which the knowledge proves the teller wise."

This occurs when the prevalent belief in an organization is that others will try to better their situation at our expense and it is therefore prudent for us to take advantage of them first.

SUMMARY

Adversarial competitiveness is a major barrier to productive work and one that leadership must combat.

- It occurs when people treat others as rivals instead of as colleagues or teammates.

- It is driven by an underlying belief that others are certain to take advantage if they get the chance, so I must take advantage first.

- It produces a "look after No. 1" culture in which each person considers only his or her own interests.

- Behavior of those seen as successful spreads quickly. If those who outdo rivals are promoted and rewarded, it sends a strong message to people that individual winning (at all costs) is expected. The saying that describes this view is, "Never give a sucker an even break."

- It results in go-and-take behavior rather than give-and-take behavior.

7

Barrier #3: Arrogant Complacency

I found it hard to get people to see a situation for what it is, and not for what it was (in the past) or what they hoped it would be.

Jack Welch, *From the Gut*

Blunders, organized blunders, do more mischief than crimes. Yes, organized carelessness is more hurtful than actual sin.

Florence Nightingale

COMPLACENCY AND WHY IT LEADS TO FAILURE

Eminent professor of engineering Henry Petroski writes, in the introduction to a book on technological disasters, that most disasters are caused by a combination of poor planning, poor design, poor testing, poor construction, and poor operation. Underlying these disasters is a phenomenon called the "complacency cycle," which Petroski explains as follows:

> Because it is impossible to test fully something so large as a bridge or a jumbo jet until it is actually built, the successful pursuit of advanced technology depends to a large extent on the validity of the design process and its assumptions. These assumptions become embodied into the end-products and systems and become fully tested only with their use.

> Breakdowns generally occur in a climate of technological complacency . . . (and then) . . . in the wake of a breakdown there tends to be renewed caution.

So Petroski likens our attitude to technology as a pendulum, with a swing toward overconfidence as the amount of time without accidents increases, and with an abrupt swing back to fearfulness once an accident occurs. These pendulum swings in confidence do not serve society well in its quest for optimum use of technology:

> If we do not become more aware of, and sensitive to, this larger cyclic phenomenon in the technological process, we can expect technology to continue to break down at its present rate.

His conclusions regarding our attitude to technology would seem to apply also to our attitude to our organizations. This complacency cycle makes the steering of an organization very hard work.

The implication is that the longer an organization goes without evaluating its outcomes and taking corrective action, the greater its complacency will become. This manifests itself as a resistance to change, specifically a resistance to making changes that will benefit stakeholders. This has serious implications for the organization's ability to set and reinforce a valid direction for itself. As predicted by the complacency cycle, the organization's eventual "failure" shakes its confidence in its decision-making process so much that it starts to doubt itself and second-guesses even the simplest decision. This makes the leader's attempts to set direction even harder.

In other words, if we do not see any risks on the horizon it is not because they are not there, but because we collectively choose not to see them. We are in the grip of complacency.

One way to prolong the warmth of self-satisfaction and complacency is to block out any information that might destroy our belief that no action is necessary. Hence the saying, "No news is good news."

That maxim is often used as a motto by ostrichlike people who do not wish to deal with issues. They make sure that no news reaches them. In this way they can claim to be prevented from making decisions by a lack of information instead of the real reason, which is that they seek to avoid responsibility even for decisions that are a core aspect of their job.

Our extreme example of this tendency is from 1902. A young Winston Churchill had accompanied British forces as a journalist on their campaign against guerrilla forces in South Africa (the Boer War). The battle at a peak called Spion Kop is going badly for British forces, in spite of their vastly superior numbers. This is mostly because of a series of poor decisions by the British generals. Churchill had been witnessing the dire results of these poor decisions from near the summit. He no doubt felt that the generals had not been receiving adequate information on the situation and consequently he rushed down the mountain to personally remedy this deficiency. According to Norman Dixon's research, instead of receiving this (admittedly unsolicited) information with gratitude, the commanding general flew into a rage and threatened to have Churchill arrested.

Feeling compelled to show that he was not against information in principle, the general dispatched a senior officer to go up the mountain and bring back news. However, he took careful steps to ensure that he would not have to face unpalatable facts. He chose as his messenger a lame man who did not know the country. Just in case he did succeed in traveling up and down the mountain, the general took the precaution of shifting his headquarters to a new location. He did this after the messenger's departure and without a word to anyone about where he was going. In this way he ensured that he did not have to hear, or react to, facts about the consequences of his decisions.

Too often in organizations today, people involved in projects and other initiatives go to great lengths to avoid having them reviewed against the original business purpose or business case. Sometime this takes the form of making sure that there is no business case!

The actions of those in the grip of complacency often follow the well-known saying "too little too late." When the evidence becomes overwhelming that the situation is headed for disaster or in fact is already a disaster, only then do they take frenzied action, with the action often bearing no relation to the solution or having any hope of improving the situation.

Churchill (perhaps drawing on his experiences as a journalist) defined three symptoms of "too little too late" in describing Britain's appeasement policies in the face of Nazi aggression in 1938:

- Refusing to act when it would save the situation

- Acting when it is too late to save the situation

- Renewing commitment to action when there is no longer any power to make it good

COMPLACENCY AND NORTEL'S FALL FROM GRACE

This principle of "No news is good news" is well illustrated by the Nortel story.

The fall from grace of telecommunications giant Nortel in the early months of 2001 sent a shockwave through the Canadian economy and the global telecom industry.

That its stock fell was not a surprise; after all, the whole telecom sector and technology stocks in general suffered. What was surprising about Nortel was that the data to predict a fall in stock price were available months earlier, but were completely ignored by Nortel management, by its hired PR people, and by financial analysts and journalists.

There was one person who had reviewed the facts, however, and downgraded Nortel stock in September 2000. He was Paul Sagawa of the Wall Street firm Sanford C. Bernstein.

Sagawa recalls that he started asking himself some fundamental questions in August 2000. He looked at the numbers, interviewed some of Nortel's key customers, and got very uncomfortable about the picture that emerged. Says Sagawa, "Nortel was announcing outrageous improvements every quarter while its biggest customers were showing signs of a slowdown." The industry's smaller, less established players were accumulating enormous debt in their rush to build high-speed networks in a saturated market. So he thought, "Nortel is making a lot of money selling stuff to companies whose credit is becoming suspect. That was the red flag."

Meanwhile, Nortel CEO John Roth was vehemently denying that there was even a cloud on the horizon, never mind a storm.

Instead of taking Nortel's word that all was well, Sagawa spent two months interviewing 59 of the company's customers in North America and Europe. He found that only four of these companies had positive cash flow. His initial view was now confirmed; there was trouble ahead for Nortel. Sagawa downgraded Nortel stock and released his report describing "a sharp deceleration in the telecommunications industry." He expected that other analysts would do their own numbers and follow his lead.

They did not. Instead, according to the *Toronto Star* of December 8, 2001, Nortel responded sharply with a PR campaign.

HOW SICK SIGMA THINKING REPLACES SIX SIGMA THINKING

Why wasn't Sagawa's analysis repeated by others? Why was his warning flag ignored? Six Sigma thinking involves a disciplined approach to improving organizational performance through collecting, analyzing, and learning from independent, objective samples of data on aspects of performance important to stakeholders. In contrast, Sick Sigma thinking involves a disciplined approach to the creation of data that conforms to predetermined positions on certain aspects of performance announced by a few influential stakeholders. Which mode of thinking was at work in Nortel and among investment analysts? (A hint: it wasn't Six Sigma.)

One reason why other analysts did not follow Sagawa, according to one source interviewed by the *Toronto Star,* was that "many analysts base their reports on information from companies, those same companies in turn base their forecasts on the analysts reports. It's a revolving, cyclical kind of mess."

Similarly, the investing public, especially in Canada, where Nortel is headquartered, didn't want to hear that the gold rush was over. Months later, Roth said: "I think almost every person on the street who had any salary or pension was asking—how do I get a piece of this?"

Inside the company, managers were not getting this information. Said a former manager who spoke to the *Star,* "Things still looked strong, we didn't hear anything about falling demand."

How does complacency manage to spread through an organization? There are behavior clues that people catch. In his book *The Five Dysfunctions of a Team,* Patrick Lencioni argues that the most damaging of these are lack of commitment and inattention to results. He explains that when (people) lack clarity and buy-in they hedge their bets and continually delay important decisions in the hopes of getting enough data to feel absolutely certain of making the right decisions. He explains that when people act as if they care more about matters other than the team's collective business goals, business results cease to be something the organization worries about.

And yet, as the story of Carl Sagawa illustrated, there is enormous potential advantage to the individual who breaks out of this "herd thinking."

For as Professor Karl Weick states: "Finally these presumed constraints, when breached by someone who is more doubting, naive or uninformed (than the rest of the community), often generate sizable advantages to the breacher."

And this is precisely what an effective leader does.

SUMMARY

Arrogant complacency is a major barrier to productive work and one that leadership must combat.

- It occurs when people don't see any risks on the horizon, not because these risks don't exist but because people collectively just choose not to see them.

- Like all the barriers it is self-perpetuating and reinforcing. If there is no need to change because we are incomparably wonderful already, it follows logically that if we see no changes ultimately being made it must mean that we really are wonderful and beyond comparison. The saying that describes this is, "No news is good news."

- Although all three barriers are deadly, arrogant complacency is particularly damaging because it prevents a critical appraisal of the organization's performance. It prevents the creation of a sense of urgency, which has been shown to be an essential ingredient for effective change.

- It results in Sick Sigma decision making replacing Six Sigma decision making.

8

Intentions: Promote Stakeholder-Focused Thinking

Not realizing who the software system's stakeholders are is the first mistake. We must recognize that "software stakeholders" extend beyond just the user.

Robin Dudash, *Software Quality,* 2003

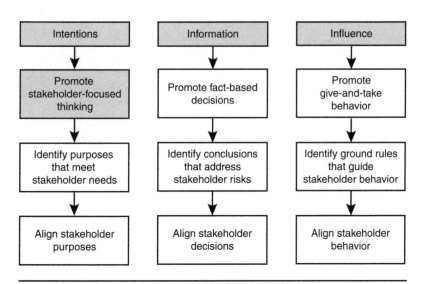

Figure 8.1   Leadership model: Intentions step 1.

A leader who believes that a project or business unit needs a defined purpose that blends all stakeholders' needs will face reluctance from those who believe that this is undesirable and may antagonize powerful stakeholders. These problematic people are adherents to "where the chief sits is the head of the table" and believe their role is to conform to what powerful stakeholders say, not dream up their own instructions. Conformity is the greatest obstacle to purpose. To combat these people, the leader must display the power of purpose to achieve superior results through aligned action.

The executive leader has a responsibility to ensure that a purpose is defined for the organization as a whole and for any subsystems for which she or he is responsible. These would include business units, work groups, and substantial projects.

If we want to do meaningful work, we must test our understanding of the overall purpose to which we should be working. We must craft a purpose for our work and test it for acceptance with the chief and any other stakeholders we have access to.

The essence of this behavior is this belief: "Everyone is the architect of their own future. Each person must take responsibility for creating, in collaboration with others, a shared future that meets their needs."

That means that we must all craft our own purpose to guide our work, and in pursuing it we create our future.

A particular responsibility is that the leader has to ensure that data on the needs and expectations of all external stakeholders are fed into the process for defining purposes. Those purposes drive all the work to be done by the organization.

This requires a rock-solid belief in the need for getting information on stakeholder needs and using this to create "intentions" that drive all work in the organization. A leader must show doggedness about sticking with a task and doing it right.

WHY WE NEED STAKEHOLDER-FOCUSED THINKING

Philosopher Robert Audi, who has explored the subject of "acting for a reason," throws light on the complex issues of why we take some actions and not others. What Audi's work explains is that to complete excellent work we need to be very clear on the needs of all the people involved. We must also have enough skills, freedom, and support to synthesize these needs into a purpose and then do the work to meet it.

An environment that enables us to do this is "stakeholder focused."

One of Audi's examples is of a woman—we'll call her Ann—who writes a letter of recommendation (for a job) to keep a promise to a friend. Audi says that in order for the letter to be written and to be of high quality, in the face of all the competing demands on Ann's time and thoughts, the purpose has to be strong enough to drive five things: the work cycle of planning, prioritizing, persisting, perspiring, and perfecting.

She must plan to do the letter. If someone asks her what she is planning to do this morning, she might answer, "I'm going to write a letter for Sally."

She must prioritize. As she goes to sit down at the computer she has in mind that it is time to keep her promise in spite of all the other items waiting for her.

She must persist. If someone walks into her office and asks her to go for an early lunch, she may reply: "No, thanks. I really must get this letter done."

She must perspire. As she starts the document and begins to type, she may struggle to get the ideas and words right. She may have to revise it many times and always be aware that the clock is ticking. She is aware that keeping her promise to Sally is the reason for sitting here rather than doing something else.

She must perfect it. As she types she reminds herself that this is a recommendation for Sally that she promised. This is why she types and reviews it carefully. If someone puts their head around the corner and says, "Aren't you finished that letter yet?" she might reply, "No, it takes time. I have to keep revising it to create the right impression. It needs to be just right."

The insight that Audi provides is that so many of our daily actions fail the test. We are not clear on why we are trying to do them, nor are we as committed to carrying them out as Ann is about her letter. We do not have a clear and compelling purpose.

In light of this, it is no mystery why so many of our intentions do not get translated into any kind of action or why, if they are started, they are quickly interrupted or replaced by other actions.

In order for Ann to perspire and perfect, she must know what the three key stakeholders' expectations are: Sally, the subject; the hiring manager, who will review it; and Ann, who provides the information and must live with her conscience if she misrepresents Sally's suitability to the potential employer.

In order for Ann to plan, to prioritize, and to persist, she must know the expectations of her boss and customers and be able to balance those with her own wants in order to justify the spending of valuable time on this, in place of other work that awaits her.

The philosophy behind "everyone is the architect of their own future" is that in order to do meaningful work we must devote effort to identifying good reasons to act, then follow through diligently on the actions to satisfy those purposes. The key point being that no one is going to tell us to do this; they are going to be asking us to act, and only action will be seen as an acceptable response. The proactive work of getting stakeholder needs and defining purpose must somehow be integrated into "action steps."

FINDING STAKEHOLDER NEEDS THAT ARE HIDDEN IN REQUESTS FOR ACTION

We tend to look at situations and decide that we cannot be the architects of our future in this area; others have all the control and we have little or none. But this is seldom really true. As long as we have our wits we can look at the options for how we handle the situation and choose the one that's likely to work out best, in light of our purpose.

This corresponds with the "habits" of Stephen Covey, whose advice to "be proactive" argues that if you want to make things happen, consciously choose a response to each situation based on what you want to achieve and then provide information and support to others so that they can do the same.

If we work in an organization, we also tend to think that executives have a lot of freedom to choose, whereas we see ourselves as having little scope. Alas, many executives also feel themselves driven by events with little scope for independent or creative action.

One executive had a refreshing attitude, one that followed the belief that everyone is the architect. This executive had a boss who was a forceful, energetic, and dynamic individual. He would tour the subsidiaries without warning to see how they were living up to the company standards—woe betide any unit that wasn't; they received a long list of to-do's and a follow-up visit.

He behaved much the same way in executive meetings, giving out to-do items to leaders of subsidiary companies. He would follow up with them too.

Most such leaders had learned to cope with their boss by passing on these requests as direct instructions to their own managers, saying, "Sorry, but it's a directive."

This particular executive used a different tactic. He used the three-step process outlined earlier. First he would make sure that he understood the idea behind the directive, what was he being asked to do, and why. He would ask questions and listen carefully as the directive was being given. While many people feel the need to understand things by asking questions, this individual could analyze the situation after the fact and piece together the thought process. For example, what was the chief talking about just before the directive was made? Were there specific reports or incidents being discussed that triggered it? Were the comments of other executives part of the chain of thought (check with them, if so).

Of course he did go back to the chief with direct questions, but he used this approach sparingly. Like all seasoned campaigners he knew that going back at a later date and asking questions can backfire. If, for example, you ask about subject "B" when the chief's mind is occupied with subject "A," you may get an unhelpful but very specific response that sends you off track.

The outcome of this first step was a knowledge of the needs of the stakeholders: the boss, customers, manufacturing plants, technologists, suppliers, and so forth.

DISCOVERING AN UNSPOKEN PURPOSE

The second step was to define a purpose that lay behind the directive but that also met the essential needs of the key stakeholders. The third step involved achieving aligned action. This had two parts, one with his own team and one with the boss.

He wanted his staff to look at how the directive could be implemented. How long would it take? How much would it cost? What would the customer/supplier impact be? What other projects would be impacted? Were there different options for doing it? He would use his understanding of what the idea was behind the directive (its purpose) in order to brainstorm with his managers and experts on alternative ways to achieve the purpose.

Then he responded to the chief. This conversation always started off by referring to the directive and describing how it could be achieved. Having got the chief's attention, the executive would skillfully bridge into the crucial second half of the conversation. He would add something like, "but I don't think you'll like the cost." At that point he would explain how the product enhancement (say) that the chief wanted required special production equipment that would have to be brought over from Sweden. The chief was likely getting disappointed during this part of the conversation, maybe a little irritated because what had seemed to him like a solution (that he was very pleased with) was turning out to be a dud after all.

Watching carefully throughout, the executive would wait for the body language of the chief to signal that he was ready to cut the idea loose and let it sink if he could see another lifeboat to jump into. Now came the masterstroke. "Of course, if what you want is to xxx (the purpose he had deduced), then there is another way we could do that." The sound of a lifeboat being launched could almost be heard.

Now followed a matter-of-fact explanation of the alternative, the best one of the several that the executive and his team had looked at. In exactly the same way as for the chief's idea, he would give the costs and benefits.

This explanation would be given in a low-key manner, with no discernable difference in enthusiasm between the discussion of the chief's idea and this new alternative. This communicated to the chief that the executive was as prepared to implement the chief's idea as he was to implement his own.

Notice that up to this point the executive has not used the word "no" nor in any way opposed the chief's idea. What the executive has done is to register three critical hits in the chief's mind. First, he showed that his idea has a downside that's important to him, in this example its cost but in other cases it could be customer satisfaction. Second, the executive had been sufficiently motivated and smart to have figured out the purpose behind the chief's idea, or at least had come close enough that the chief could adjust it and then articulate his purpose clearly.

Third, the executive had been sufficiently supportive of the chief's purpose to find a better way to achieve it.

ACHIEVING ALIGNED ACTION

Now we have reached the last step. At this point the chief is still in the position of decision maker; he can choose freely between the alternatives on merit. He feels good. He now has a purpose in place of a specific idea, and he has a way to implement it that his executive came up with on his own.

How clever the chief has been. By challenging his executive, he has got him to propose this excellent plan. At this point he may ask the executive's opinion as to which course is best. There may be further detail or risks that he should hear about. Perhaps the executive will add that pursuing the alternative will allow them to make better use of in-house expertise, enabling them to still deliver on other projects that would be jeopardized under the chief's idea.

What the executive knew was that involving the originator of a request in the decision of what to do about it is a critical step. It gives completion and makes the individual, whether corporate chief, customer, or entry-level employee feel that their contribution has been recognized. This feeling of vindication and empowerment can free them from the desire to push their request forward as the only means to get satisfaction.

The executive's process worked well for him and can, with suitable adaptation, work equally well for anyone who wishes to be the architect of their own future. Of course, this process involves upfront effort. But one can also easily see that it saves significant downstream effort. Trying to implement an ill-conceived idea will take much more effort than the investment required to "fix the idea" upfront.

In particular for a individual in a management position, with responsibility for allocating people to projects and balancing budgets and workloads, this is a crucial process to master. Yet it is true that doing this for every request may be impossible. Yet for projects where significant resources will be invested, we must find a way.

And only a leader can do this with any chance of success. A project manager is usually appointed too late, and is usually poorly placed to do so, both organizationally and in terms of time. They are expected to jump into action.

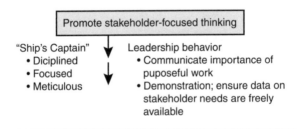

Figure 8.2　Summary of Intentions step 1.

SUMMARY

The Intentions theme starts when the leader recognizes that organizations exist to serve stakeholders and then acts accordingly.

- A particular responsibility that a leader has is to ensure that data on the needs and expectations of all stakeholders are fed into the process for defining purposes, which drive all the work to be done by the organization.

- The time and effort to do this must often be found by the leader using creativity, because the stakeholders themselves will be looking for action, not synthesis of needs into purposes.

- Above all it requires the leader to have the will to define their own valid purpose in the face of powerful forces that want them to adopt other purposes. The saying that describes this, "Everyone is the architect of their own future."

9

Intentions: Identify Purposes That Meet Stakeholder Needs

Purpose is in the woodwork of the organization, is not set or created as much as it is recognized and discovered.
Jim Collins and Jerry Porras, *Built to Last*

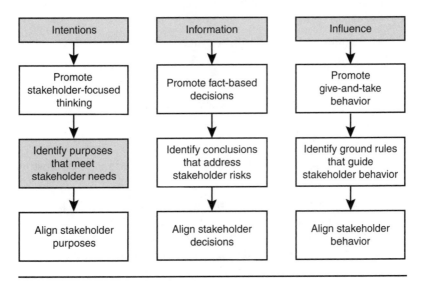

Figure 9.1   Leadership model: Intentions step 2.

PURPOSE AS DNA OF SUCCESSFUL ORGANIZATION

Purpose is the DNA of a successful organization or project. Mistakes in purpose definition lead to efforts that drift further and further off track with each day and each dollar spent. If an organization has a purpose defined for itself, then everything else flows from this: organization structure, reward systems, everything.

As a variation on an adage says: "A stitch of purpose in time saves nine." In other words, defining clear and compelling purposes for any undertaking, before starting work, saves much misunderstanding and wasted effort.

As Sir John Harvey-Jones states, most organization failures occur not because of mistakes or screw-ups, but because the organization is not going anywhere, and no organization can survive by standing still in today's world.

It is no accident that the first of quality guru Dr. W. Edwards Deming's "14 points" for the transformation of organizations deals with purpose. Deming's questions for management start (in *Out of the Crisis*) as follows:

Has your company established an organizational purpose?

- Will it stay fixed, or change as presidents come and go? (And who does your president and board report to?)

- Do all your employees know about this raison d'être?

- How many believe it, to the extent that it affects their work?

Deming gives an insight into why this cascading of purpose is so crucial:

A software programmer learns, after she has finished a task, that she programmed very well according to the specifications as given to her, but they were deficient. If she had only known the purpose of the program, she could have done it right for the purpose, even through the specifications were deficient.

THE LONG-TERM IMPACT OF A CLEAR PURPOSE ON MARKET PERFORMANCE

An excellent book was published in 2001 by Jim Collins, coauthor of the classic *Built to Last*. Collins and his team spent several years sifting through the financial results of U.S.-listed public companies to identify those that had transformed themselves financially from "ugly ducklings" into "beautiful swans." The new book is aptly titled *Good to Great.*

Collins and his team found 11 such good-to-great companies from a range of industries that had at one time in the past performed at an average level in their industry and subsequently had taken off in an upward trend lasting more than a decade. They set about studying these companies through publicly available research data, interviews, and comparisons with industry competitors that had once been similar in performance but had failed to transform their results to the same extent as the study group.

Collins found these companies developed purposes that were "simple, crystalline concepts that flow from a deep understanding about what you can be the best in the world at, what drives your economic engine and what you are deeply passionate about."

For example, Abbott determined that its purpose was "to create a product portfolio that lowers the cost of healthcare." This was based on the realization that Abbott could not be the world leader at developing pharmaceutical drugs even though, at the time Abbott made its decision, the majority of its revenue came from pharmaceuticals. Consequently Abbott focused its skills and knowledge into creating healthcare services in areas like nutritional services, diagnostics, and hospital supply services.

Similarly, Walgreens decided that its purpose was to become "America's convenience drugstore." This led Walgreens to develop corner pharmacies in neighborhoods throughout the United States and to cluster these stores within a small radius linked by a distribution system to ensure that Walgreens's wide range of products were always in stock.

Purpose influences both the design of a system/structure and its evolution. The two examples we look at next show what happens when something is designed to meet a clear purpose, and what happens when a complex organization evolves around a central purpose. The story of MIT's legendary Building 20 illustrates the impact on design of a clear purpose.

THE IMPACT OF PURPOSE ON THE DESIGN OF A STRUCTURE: MIT'S BUILDING 20

Building 20 at the Massachusetts Institute of Technology is a structure with a unique history. It illustrates that when we construct something well for a purpose, and if that purpose remains valid with stakeholders, the structure will endure.

Building 20 is only known by its number; it has no name. It had no prestigious architect, and even its most ardent admirers will admit it's ugly. It provides a quarter-million square feet of research space on MIT's campus. It is affiliated with no specific department or school of study. It has few amenities and almost no controls. Furthermore, Building 20 has been due for demolition its whole life.

Yet few buildings can claim such a rich history of nurturing world-changing research.

It was designed for the wartime development of radar in 1943, and afterward it housed MIT's first interdisciplinary laboratory, the research laboratory of electronics that founded much of modern communications science. In the 1950s such companies as Digital got started there, and in the 1960s a group operating from Building 20, the unlikely named Model Railroad Club, helped found the practice of computer hacking.

And yet if Building 20 seems to have been successful by accident, it was an accident driven by purpose.

Legend has it that it was designed in an afternoon by MIT grad Don Whiston and was built in six months using timber because of wartime steel shortages.

The United States needed to develop radar, and a multidisciplinary team of physicists was instructed to assemble at MIT to get the job done, a project of similar scope to the Manhattan Project, which developed the atomic bomb.

Consequently the structure was designed by a researcher to provide a flexible environment for multidisciplinary research. Its wood construction, which gives it unique strength and easy expansion for research teams, is in fact against building codes and had to be given an exemption by the city. Its "due for demolition" status was tacked on to the exemption in 1943 and has remained in force ever since.

Building 20 has survived because it is an ideal environment for research and, at MIT at least, researchers are stakeholders with clout. Perhaps luckily for the researchers, the replacement cost has always been too high for other stakeholders to justify its removal on aesthetic grounds.

The building is made for free thinking, aided by its ample daylight, for the exchange of ideas between researchers by its numerous long corridors, and the immediate testing of ideas by adaptable space, and open access services. As one researcher said, "It's the only building on campus you can cut with a saw."

Architect Stewart Brand perhaps best summarizes why it works for its occupants: "You feel yourself walking in historic footsteps in pursuit of technical solutions that might be elegant precisely because they are quick and dirty—and that describes the building, elegant because it is quick and dirty."

Building 20 is unique mostly because of its size and the fact that it sits on MIT's campus, but it is in fact a typical example of a class of structures that are found all over the world and act as homes for innovation. Nowadays these are known as "the garages of Silicon Valley." The most famous of these is the small garage in Palo Alto, CA, where in 1939 two youngsters named William Hewlett and David Packard founded the firm of Hewlett-Packard. Not surprisingly, this garage is a California state monument!

A fascinating aside is to note that the firm that started in Building 20, Digital, and the one that started in the garage, HP, have joined forces, in part, their leaders claim, because of their compatible cultures, both of which were formed in unpretentious wooden buildings. It is as if their original purpose, which flourished in their humble freedom-enhancing buildings, shaped their cultures.

THE IMPACT OF PURPOSE ON THE EVOLUTION OF A STRUCTURE: THE MARSHALL PLAN

A remarkable example of the power of purpose to influence the evolution of a complex organization is the story of the Marshall Plan. *Marshall Plan* is a term meaning a transfer of resources that produces effective results. Politicians and economists often use the term: "What we need is a Marshall Plan for this region/industry/country." In an article in the *Harvard Business Review* (2004), Peter Drucker credits the Marshall Plan with driving the growth and prosperity of Europe, and the world economy.

The Marshall Plan itself, proposed in 1947 by Secretary of State George Marshall, was enacted in 1948 by the U.S. Congress as a bold initiative to directly assist the rebuilding of Western Europe, many of whose cities and factories lay in ruins. The purpose of the Marshall Plan was "to restore the economies of the nations of Western Europe." The Economic Cooperation Administration (ECA) was set up to implement the initiative, which involved the transfer of U.S. funds to Europe in order to accomplish the purpose.

Nobel Prize winner Herbert Simon writes (in *The Sciences of the Artificial*) that there were at least six alternative schemes proposed for distributing funds and that these all appeared in the legislation and in the operations of the ECA in its early days. These options ranged from the "screening of shopping lists for materials" drawn up by European countries, to project-by-project evaluations, to collaborative planning by European nations, to a country-by-country trade gap focus. The most sophisticated plan was the proposal that there should be a policy-making body for Western Europe and that an administrative body following those policies should manage the funds.

Simon reports that had all the options been implemented with equal vigor, massive confusion would have resulted and that in fact this very nearly happened. What saved the Marshall Plan from ending in the kind of failure that is all too common for "grand schemes" was that its purpose was clear. It was clear enough for everyone to understand, and this common understanding facilitated action rather than paralysis, which led to better understanding. The options that emerged as dominant from the original proposals were European collaborative planning and individual country trade gap closure. In hindsight this is hardly surprising because these are the two options that most closely support the recognition and restoration of "nations." There is also no doubt that the ECA set Europe on the path to greater collaboration, first in the guise of the European Community and more recently through the European Union (EU). Also of note is that the European Union has now implemented the policy-making body and the administrative body first proposed under the Marshall Plan.

Few would question the effectiveness of the Marshall Plan in achieving its purpose, nor that it laid the foundation for the most significant change in Europe, and one of the most significant in the world in the 20th century.

Witness the speed with which countries of Eastern Europe applied for membership in the early years of this century. To these nations, applying for EU membership is a defining vision for the future, much like immigration to America was for individuals in the early 20th century.

It is interesting to note that in mid-2005 much confusion arose after voters in France and the Netherlands rejected a draft European Constitution. Part of the confusion came from the fact that no one is really sure how the votes affect the future of the European Union. Yet from this analysis of the roots of the Union it is evident that the forerunner ECA had a purpose of mutual aid and cooperation between *nations,* not individual Europeans.

In light of this it is perhaps not surprising that ordinary citizens have not wholeheartedly embraced the EU as a structure because they were never intended to do so. It was a tool for their elected leaders to use in pursuit of economic growth, stability, and, most importantly, peaceful coexistence.

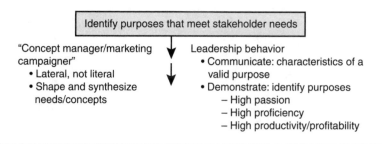

Figure 9.2   Summary of Intentions step 2.

SUMMARY

The second part of the leadership theme of Intentions is the identification of purposes. Crucial aspects of this work are:

- Communicating an appreciation of what a purpose is and why it is necessary. The saying that describes this is, "A stitch (of purpose) in time saves nine."

- Describing what the organization does in simple, practical terms with no more words than are necessary. The description must embody a deep understanding of what the organization is passionate about, what it can be best at, and what drives its economic engine.

10

Intentions: Align Stakeholder Purposes

Leaders seek audiences. Emperors give audiences.

Marshall McLuhan

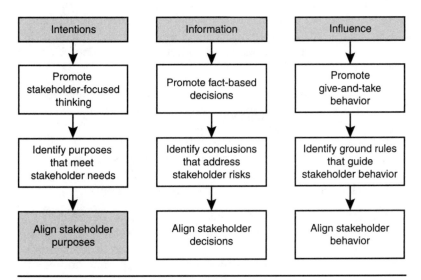

Figure 10.1 Leadership model: Intentions step 3.

PURPOSE SPREADS BY SEIZING OUR IMAGINATION

This step of the process involves getting all stakeholders to adopt the purpose, align their efforts behind it, and implement aligned actions so that efforts will work in harmony rather than at cross-purposes. The key to this is that the purpose must be easy to "transmit."

As the saying asserts: United we stand, divided we fall. When success depends on actions by many people, unity must be achieved around a common purpose and plan.

Purpose is an idea. To be powerful, an idea needs to capture the imagination. How does this happen? Evolutionary thinker Richard Dawkins (who wrote *The Selfish Gene*) describes a model for the spread and success of ideas through the human population. He calls such ideas "memes," a name derived from the Greek for "imitate" because they spread from person to person through imitation.

Norbert Wiener, in his landmark book *Cybernetics,* explains simply how we can get to learn people's ideas without needing to hear or understand their words. Hypothetically, this could occur at a meeting in a far-off land with someone who did not speak or understand any language in common with us.

> All I need to do is to be alert to those moments when he shows signs of emotion or interest. I then cast my eyes around, perhaps paying special attention to the direction of his glance and fix in my memory what I see or hear. It will not be long before I discover the things which seem important to him, not because he has communicated them to me by language, but because I myself have observed them.

Dawkins argues that our "mental computing" resources are scarce. The brain and the body that controls it cannot do more than few things at once. If a meme is to dominate the attention of a brain, it must do so at the expense of rival memes. Other commodities for which memes compete are radio and TV time, billboard space, newspaper column inches, and library shelf space.

A meme, he says, can be as complex as Darwin's theory or as simple as a distinctive musical phrase from Beethoven's *Ninth Symphony.* Successful memes are distinctive enough to retain their identity when passed on and appealing enough to be the "mind-share" leader among similar ideas circulating within people's minds.

An example of something that was designed to be distinctive and appealing is Beethoven's *Ninth Symphony*. The status of the *Ninth* as an icon of classical music is unquestionable. In order that listeners could enjoy the entire work at one sitting, the 74-minute symphony was used to set the standard capacity for the compact disc.

In a history of "Ode to Joy," historian Esteban Buch showed that far from the *Ninth Symphony*'s becoming an anthem by accident, it was always designed to be just that.

Beethoven, claims the historian, was an enthusiastic player in the game of national prestige and was keen to position himself as the most important composer in Europe. So for the Congress of Vienna in 1814, he composed a piece that contained a hymn to European ideals. The *Ninth Symphony* was subsequently based on this model, appearing a decade later, with its effect on public consciousness refined and strengthened.

In the nearly 200 years since its first appearance, the *Ninth Symphony* has strengthened its hold on the collective consciousness of Europeans, as evidenced by the fact that it has, for 30 years, been the official anthem of the European Union.

PURPOSE AS A MENTAL SWISS ARMY KNIFE FOR ORGANIZING AND PRIORITIZING WORK

What makes a purpose so appealing to us?

The answer is simple. If people believe that the organization that they are working with is structured around a purpose and, in the absence of more specific detail, that they should focus on helping achieve that purpose, purpose becomes a very useful tool. Like Deming's software programmer they can produce a good-quality result even if the "specifications" are deficient. In this sense, purpose becomes like an intellectual Swiss army knife for cutting through complexity, confusion, and contradiction. Such a "knife" is an invaluable tool for people to carry.

The "Trouble Shooter," Sir John Harvey-Jones tells each of the 30 or so organizations that he coached of the vital importance of staying focused. Focus everyone, he says, on the two or three things that the organization should be doing right now; concentrate until they are done. "You need to spend a lot of time stopping people running off down by-ways."

The common thread that runs through all the examples in *Good to Great* is summarized by author Jim Collins: "We should not add these findings to what we are already doing and make ourselves even more overworked, but to realize that much of what we're doing is at best a waste of energy. If we organized our work time around applying these principles and pretty much ignored or stopped doing everything else—our lives would be simpler and our results vastly improved." What comes through consistently from these companies is what Collins calls "a fanatical adherence to their concept—anything that does not fit—we will not do."

This discipline of continuously communicating purpose, conducting a dialogue with stakeholders about its implications, and summarizing their feedback and concerns is the essence of the intentions theme of leadership.

LEADERS COMMUNICATE PURPOSE EVERY DAY IN A DIFFERENT WAY

A powerful example of purpose and what can happen when we implement it is given by Collins. It concerns a high school cross-country running team. The coaches who took over the struggling team came up with a new mission: "We run best at the end." They backed this up with their actions. Dispensing with "fun events" at which the club tried to attract new members and keep existing ones, the coaches reinforced the idea that "running *is* fun."

This concept of alignment of people with purpose is stressed by Collins as being of utmost importance. He talks about two aspects: moving the "right people" in and moving the "wrong people" out. By declaring a clear purpose with commitment, people can be asked to make a choice. Begin the transformation by first getting the right people on the bus and into the right seats. Speed up the transformation by getting the wrong people off the bus, having first made sure they're not just in the wrong seat. (These would be the runners who don't want to run fastest at the end.)

Instead of tracking runners' times at various distances, the coaches tracked times at various stages in races so that people could see for themselves that "we run best at the end."

This motto went right to the core of distance running, the ability to keep going, both physically and mentally, and yet hold something in reserve to fight for places as the race comes to a close. By focusing on this simple message, the coaches focused their young athletes in a way that would either make them improve or make them want to leave the team.

What Collins calls the "flywheel" effect kicked in after only a season or two. Runners lined up to get in to the club. The club won several state cross-country titles and went on to win many other accolades.

This impact of clear purpose is also apparent in the NASA of the 1960s and early 1970s. In 1970, Tom Taormina was a young quality control engineer with Ford Aerospace assigned to work on the Apollo program. Taormina took shifts at Mission Control during spaceflight.

When the now famous message, "Houston we've got a problem," was broadcast from Apollo 13 by astronaut Jack Swigert, the routine of Apollo missions was completely changed.

Writing in *Quality Progress* magazine, Taormina recalls acting as a willing scribe, assisting the teams of engineers and specialists involved in developing the emergency rescue plan. He also recalls that the team never seemed to doubt that their preparation would result in a successful outcome.

He recalls that the efforts of hundreds of people working in the team seemed to be focused on the words of the late president John Kennedy: "This nation should commit itself to achieving the goal, before this decade is out, of landing a man on the moon and returning him safely to earth."

Taormina's view is of how clear, concise, and resonant this was in the mind of everyone. "It was at the center of every activity I performed in the 4 years I worked at NASA and it was a profound lesson that common purpose could result in otherwise impossible outcomes."

THE IMPACT OF COMMON PURPOSE ON ALIGNED ACTIONS

As an illustration of transmitting purpose and getting aligned action, the story of one company's validation of its mission serves well.

Poised to enter new markets and challenging for a leadership position in its existing market, a large manufacturer decided to launch this change by developing a new vision and mission.

Before going further, the executives decided to get feedback from employees and selected customers. The employees were consulted via focus group sessions held in every plant and at headquarters; small groups discussed the draft statement and provided anonymous feedback.

When the facilitators gave the summary of the feedback to management, it showed that some changes needed to be made. The employees proved extremely forthright and insightful, putting their finger on the key issues, not only with the words themselves but the implications of pursuing the path stated in the purpose.

"Take the flowery language out and get down to the core," suggested one employee. Others showed that they understood the importance of getting the words to say exactly what was meant.

"So that the maintenance guy, in the plant at 4 A.M. on Saturday, can look at it and say—yep, that's why I'm here!"

"At our own level we make our own mission for our crew—but this mission needs to filter down from this into all the little groups, and right now this mission is not very focused!"

"This is 180 degrees from where we are today!"

Yet others pointed out the dangers of adapting a purpose/mission and not being committed to it.

"Don't put this out unless you're committed to it. It'll hurt us."

"It's all fine and good as long as we see things to back it up."

In addition to the oral feedback, participants were asked to consider some statements and give answers on a five-point scale ranging from "strongly disagree" to "strongly agree." One such statement was "This purpose accurately describes why we are in business." Approximately half of the respondents disagreed with this statement.

The management team, to its great credit, used this feedback as an opportunity to review and reconsider the new purpose. In many ways the employee feedback mirrored some of the managers' own reservations. In particular, they were concerned that any move to broaden the range of products and technologies in the manufacturing plants would erode the so-far winning formula of high-quality, high-volume, and low-cost manufacture.

Often a management team faced with a self-imposed deadline for completing a task will cut off its debate about fundamental issues. By seeking wider views, this management team could see that significant issues still needed to be worked through.

In working through the issues, the management team concluded that the company would have to be restructured to form a group of companies that would have a wider purpose, leaving the original company focused on its core products. They also implemented a strategic planning process for this group of companies; it identified priorities for the coming three years based on each company's mission and strategic opportunities. In this way priorities and objectives were aligned across the group and also within each company. Departments at the head office and plants were on the same page and the potential for working at cross-purposes was greatly reduced. They also chose to implement a balanced scorecard, with key performance indicators to help them measure and plan their progress toward achievement of their purpose and vision.

The balanced scorecard approach, made popular by Robert Kaplan and David Norton, involves the definition of a set of measures that reflect all areas of performance that are critical to strategic success. These include not only measures of financial performance, the lagging indicators, but also measures of the drivers, the leading indicators of future financial performance.

The company identified a number of lagging and leading indicators in such key areas as cost, quality, market share, customer satisfaction, and employee satisfaction. These reinforced the organization's focus on existing strengths. In addition, the company developed measures for innovation. This work helped executives better define and communicate what kind of innovation outcomes they needed and what kind of infrastructure was needed to make this possible. This greatly assisted communication about these areas, which, as Kaplan and Norton found, is the biggest advantage of balanced scorecard implementations.

The manufacturer developed its measures in line with Kaplan and Norton's findings of balanced scorecard companies, of approximately 25 measures, typically 5 financial, 5 customer, 10 internal (or process), and 5 covering learning and growth. The internal (process) perspective has more measures because it is the critical linkage point in transforming intangible assets (ideas, skills, energy) into tangible outcomes (customer retention, market growth, financial results).

The strategic planning process with a balanced scorecard was a leadership tool the group CEO could use to hold structured dialogues with company leaders about their mission and the direction and extent of growth both in terms of bottom-line numbers and capabilities. This created a common mind-set around the future, the ultimate stage in alignment of purpose.

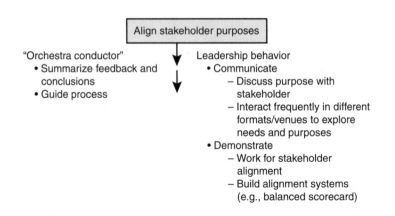

Figure 10.2 Summary of Intentions step 3.

SUMMARY

The third and final part of the Intentions theme concerns the leadership role of aligning stakeholder purposes. It involves:

- Ensuring that the purpose set for the organization is one that all stakeholders are committed to and that will drive all priorities, plans, and actions. The saying that describes this is, "United we stand, divided we fall."

- Making it meaningful for all members of the organization. It should be capable of being interpreted by anyone doing any task in the organization, and it should provide guidance. Reflecting on it will give sufficient reasons to either do or not do a task.

- Discussing organizational purpose at every opportunity with stakeholders and expressing interest in and solid support for their purpose. This gradually aligns purposes in an indirect way through give-and-take.

- Create systems that help maintain alignment of purpose and priorities.

11

Information: Promote Fact-Based Decisions

Without check-ins to re-examine the plan as events unfold, the executive has no way of knowing which events really matter and which are noise.

Peter Drucker

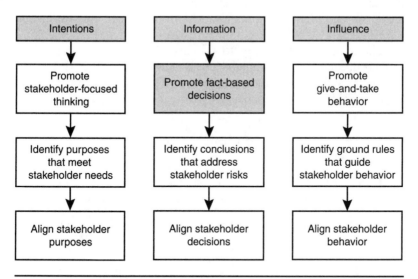

Figure 11.1 Leadership model: Information step 1.

IMPROVEMENT REQUIRES WILLINGNESS TO REVIEW DATA ON OUTCOMES

Even after the purpose has been defined, there is no guarantee that subsequent plans and actions will be aligned with it. As with most things in this world, events do not always unfold as they should. With layers of interpretation, lots of people and lots of plans and agendas involved, it would be surprising indeed if all the activity in any system linked up with its purpose and remained so over time.

Consequently someone must stand back from the day-to-day hustle and bustle and take a hard look at the behavior of the system and its results to check whether its "purpose as implemented" matches its "purpose as intended."

Reviews provide opportunities for improvement action for managers and individuals alike. But to take advantage of these opportunities, people must feel secure, not threatened. Here the leader's own behavior plays a critical role.

There is an old saying: "If you are not part of the solution, you are part of the problem." Improvement requires regular reviews of actual versus intended outcomes, which can occur only when all stakeholders visibly participate in an open-minded way.

The most effective way to put a project back on track was defined decades ago by social scientist Kurt Lewin. It is driven by "learning" and is sometimes called "action learning." In this process the stakeholders are not mere passengers; they are the crew. Lewin's steps are:

- A review is conducted when the leader perceives that it is necessary.

- Objective data are collected and a tentative diagnosis is made by the leader or someone he or she appoints.

- These data are fed back to all key individuals and groups who are stakeholders.

- A joint diagnosis of the situation (which supersedes all previous conclusions) is made by the stakeholders.

- A joint action plan and goals are set.

- Action is taken.

- The evaluation process is repeated at a predetermined time to check that things are now on track.

So unless a leader is prepared for the project's purpose to drift, he or she must check the actions against purpose at regular intervals. It is like a ship's captain checking the actual course against the charted course.

THE IMPORTANCE OF REVIEW BASED ON DATA

In the event that the evaluation reveals a significant difference between the intended purpose and the implemented purpose, the leader's responsibility is to help the organization take appropriate action.

An evaluation consists of comparing the stated purpose and the purpose deduced from the actions completed. Based on the gap between these two and the capability of the organization to close this gap, a course of action is taken to reconcile the intended purpose with the allocation of resources.

This is not merely an evaluation of whether or not the plan is being followed. It is certainly true that having a plan and following it are important behaviors that are part of the evaluation, but still only a part. What the evaluation is looking at is the extent to which the system is on track in its purpose, not only in its plan. In other words, the plan may have looked as good as anyone could make it when things got started. But in the light of current knowledge and actual outcomes, we may find that the plan was never going to be good enough to achieve the purpose.

As Sir John Harvey-Jones points out, when organizations get into trouble the people managing them almost never question what they're doing but assume more effort is needed, and so they work harder and bury the organization even quicker.

Few authors have spelled out the advantages of using data to review projects and processes better than Dr. Edwards Deming. His 14 points advocate that managers must be part of the solution. He sets out a logical series of steps based on data-based review that leads to continuously improving performance:

1. Provide training for employees on standards of what is acceptable work and what is not, based on customer needs and organizational purpose. *Are there instances where people do not seem to know what is acceptable work?*

2. Build processes with process control feedback loops to performers based on samples, instead of rework loops based on 100 percent inspection of completed work. *Are there adequate feedback*

loops to workers that enable them to spot problems early and correct them effectively?

3. Identify the causes of built-in delays and mistakes and create a system or plan that is free of them. *Are there system/structure problems that contribute to the difficulty of getting quality work done, and what action is being taken on these?*

4. Provide opportunities for self-improvement to all and coaching where data shows individuals are statistically outside the statistical bell curve. *Are there people whose performance is outside the bell curve, and how are they being assisted to improve?*

5. Communicate regularly to everyone the results of improvement efforts and plans to remove obstacles and help people work smarter. *Is there a clear understanding of the improvement plan, why it is necessary, and how everyone contributes?*

6. Plan organizational performance using historical averages, and set goals based on explicit knowledge of process capability. *Are the current plans and goals realistic given previous data (both operating plan and improvement plan)?*

PERSONAL COMMITMENT TO BLAME-FREE, EFFECTIVE, ACTION-ORIENTED REVIEWS

In order to gain anything like open-minded participation, the leader must be able to make three promises to those who participate in reviews. These are:

1. Singling people out for punishment or censure is not the focus of the evaluation.

2. An effective process that takes full account of all relevant data to reach conclusions will be used.

3. Clear decisions that they can understand and implement will result from the evaluation.

It is no coincidence that Jim Collins's research showed that good-to-great transformations were led by people who had a blame-free style. Collins found that the leaders of these companies believed that they should look out the window to give credit for success, but look in the mirror to award blame for shortcomings.

As an example of how a leader can convince people that they are better off participating than not we look at a successful TV series made in Britain.

A prominent business executive, John Harvey-Jones, retired as chairman of Imperial Chemical Industries (ICI), a major-league company with headquarters in the United Kingdom. Harvey-Jones, because of his success in growing ICI into a world-class organization and because of his down-to-earth personality and excellent communication skills, was in the early 1990s the best-known British business executive and arguably the most respected. The BBC approached Harvey-Jones, or "Sir John" as he was universally referred to, to make a TV series featuring him as a consultant providing advice to troubled British companies. A number of companies in the private sector, some of them very famous names in Britain, volunteered to take part. Surprisingly to producers, a large number of public sector organizations also volunteered to participate, from such fields as law enforcement and medicine.

Several series of the shows, called *The Troubleshooter,* were made and were well received by the public. The material from these shows was also written up in book form.

During his visits to these organizations, he would not only gather information but also work to persuade the executives to see the exercise in the right context. He would try to persuade them, by sharing his philosophy and experiences, to participate and be part of the solution.

Sir John's expressed philosophy gave explicit reasons why people should participate in an open-minded way.

First, decisions and actions that in hindsight can be judged to be "a wrong turn" are seldom caused by ineptitude but are a byproduct of the inherent difficulty of predicting business environments.

Second, however tempting it may be to gloss over the past and avoid painful self-doubts and remorse, the only way to identify the right corrective actions is to be ruthlessly honest.

Third, our natural tendency is to be overoptimistic, which leads us to make a few small changes and then wait to see how much impact they have had before taking further steps. While this may be fine when reviews are held regularly and performance is kept on course, it is dangerously timid in situations where no comprehensive reviews have occurred for some time. In such cases, sometimes referred to as "strategic drift," where a noticeable gap has been widening between stakeholder expectations of performance on the one hand and what the organization is delivering on the other, the likelihood is high that some type of drastic action will be necessary to realign the two. Senior management should be prepared for this. Sir John set the expectations by asking, "Do you have the heart to make really big changes?"

These points communicate a credible version of the leader's "three promises" of reviews: they are not blame-focused, they involve a comprehensive data-based process, and they lead to clear, effective decisions.

For senior managers, Sir John emphasized the first of these points, and he displayed a particularly skillful way of doing this. He went to great lengths to put past decisions in the most charitable light possible by emphasizing the difficulty of the decision and the efforts undertaken to make the best decision in the circumstances:

"when disaster struck the family did not stand idly by"

"it must have cost the Letts family a tremendous amount of agonizing to face up to the inevitability of"

"to their credit the family bravely faced the facts and sold"

"look some uncomfortable facts in the face"

These descriptions of people's past behavior are very important, beyond the removal of people's fears of being blamed. Harvey-Jones was setting the stage for the kind of behaviors he needed to see from managers by providing them with examples from their past where they demonstrated these behaviors. For instance, if he believed they needed to face facts and sell off a company, he described to them a similar situation where they did just that. This also helped build people's self-belief that they could manage their way out of difficulties, because an enterprise that feels beset by problems often starts to feel that it has "lost it" and is incapable of taking the right actions. This loss of self-confidence can be fatal.

Sir John's success rate in getting organizations to take action was very high. Some took longer to decide and act than others. In a recent interview, Sir John revealed that he still meets once a year with all the organizations he advised and that almost all the issues that he had highlighted have been addressed in one way or another. Only one organization, a world-famous brand of children's toys, had gone out of business. It had started to act but alas too late to stave off financial collapse. In my view this successful record by Sir John has a great deal to do with his ability to get people to be part of the solution, as evidenced by the fact that he has an ongoing relationship with these companies.

WHY DEAD RECKONING IS OFTEN DEAD WRONG

To break down complacency, the leader can also point out that people's general sense of where they are now based on where they have been is highly unreliable.

In many ways the parallels between people's behavior when organizationally lost and when physically lost, say in the outdoors, is striking. Those who do not want to have a review are like people who are content to hike the wilderness using only dead reckoning to check their position, rather than checking landmarks or using global positioning system (GPS) to fix their position objectively.

Studies have shown that humans have no innate sense of direction, unlike birds, but rely on working out where they are relative to landmarks. This is why, without points of reference, people can be a long way away from where they think they are and not know it.

Ken Hill of Saint Mary's University in Halifax, Nova Scotia, is a world authority on how people get lost and how to find them. As he explained to Jeffery Clugston, writing in *Canadian Geographic* magazine: "I learned that people can get lost so incredibly quickly: by and large people underestimate the effort that is required for dead reckoning—knowing your location and direction/speed of travel." And humans, according to Clugston's research, just don't have the right skills for dead reckoning.

"Science has known for half a century that humans have no innate sense of direction. Instead, we orient ourselves by environmental cues: the sun, the stars, prominent landmarks." This situation is further compounded by people's natural stubbornness, which results in many people, especially experienced outdoorsmen, denying they are lost and refusing to backtrack. Perhaps the old joke about men never asking for directions is true! They can become convinced they are heading in the right direction, steadfastly ignoring mounting evidence to the contrary.

Even when people do finally recognize that they are lost, there is a further problem. People can easily become disoriented and, as a result, are unable to think logically. Often this leads to a decision to press on in order to somehow get themselves unlost, which compounds the difficulty of their situation. They become more tired, more disoriented, and more likely further and further away from help and familiar landmarks. As a result, the distances lost people can cover routinely surprises searchers. Clugston points out the heart of the problem and the lengths people go to overcome their natural weaknesses. "A false sense of certainty can affect even trained searchers who know the phenomenon. Some have taken to carrying two compasses. The back-up compass defends them against the bull-headed belief that their sense of direction is right and the first compass must be broken."

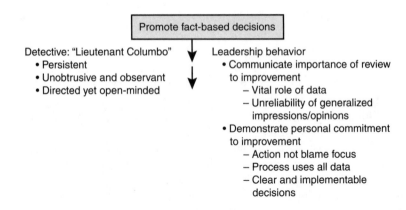

Promote fact-based decisions

Detective: "Lieutenant Columbo"
• Persistent
• Unobtrusive and observant
• Directed yet open-minded

Leadership behavior
• Communicate importance of review
  to improvement
  – Vital role of data
  – Unreliability of generalized
    impressions/opinions
• Demonstrate personal commitment
  to improvement
  – Action not blame focus
  – Process uses all data
  – Clear and implementable
    decisions

Figure 11.2 Summary of Information step 1.

SUMMARY

The first part of the Information theme is promoting fact-based decisions, which involves:

• Convincing people that reviews are necessary. Decisions must be made with stakeholders in mind, and they must use objective data.

• Explaining that over time organizations lose their way and get off track. Objective, open-minded reviews get things back on track, but this requires all those involved to participate. The saying that describes this is, "If you are not part of the solution, you are part of the problem."

• Reassuring people that punishment or blame is not the focus of the review, that an effective process will be used to form conclusions from all the data, and that decisions will be made.

12

Information: Identify Conclusions That Address Stakeholder Risks

You are neither right nor wrong because the crowd disagrees with you. You are right because your data and reasoning are right.
Warren Buffet

Unless you are communicating settled findings use labels only to tell the viewer how to read the data (not what to read into it).
Edward R. Tufte

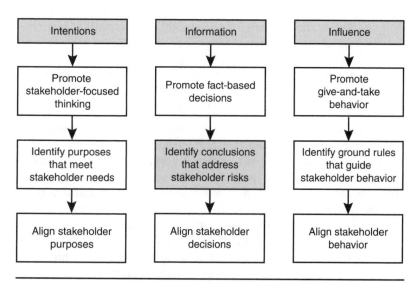

Figure 12.1 Leadership model: Information step 2.

How does a leader ensure that the process will reveal the key conclusions?

Peter Senge expressed it in his learning discipline, which he called "mental models," which involved holding conversations that bring to the surface people's assumptions, separate data from interpretation, and create shared mental models to underpin strategies.

As the saying goes: "Facts are stubborn things." A review that focuses exclusively on sharing all the facts of the matter usually leads to conclusions accepted by all.

The ideal process is described by the most logical of all fictional characters, Sherlock Holmes. He describes two critical steps in understanding data; namely, sifting the data to separate the crucial facts, and then seeing the implications.

SIFT THE DATA TO SEPARATE THE CRUCIAL FACTS

The first step is to sift the data. As Holmes explained to Dr. Watson:

Sometimes the art of the reasoner should be used for the sifting of details rather than the gathering of fresh evidence. We are suffering from a plethora of surmise, conjecture and hypothesis. The difficulty is to detach the framework of fact, absolute undeniable fact, from embellishments.

Having gathered these facts, Watson, I smoked several pipes over them, trying to separate those which were crucial from those which were merely incidental.

We need to build up a portrait of the system by adding and rearranging data, stopping when we reach the point where the picture stabilizes and does not change significantly with the addition of more data. A cartoonist who captures a situation with a few well-drawn lines can only dilute the impact by drawing in more detail that is irrelevant to the message or caption.

One key to success in characterizing the system's behavior is to stick to objective, factual descriptions of events and occurrences. This ensures that people's minds are not derailed by going into a blame or defense mode, for once this takes hold the process is doomed.

The most effective language for describing the system behavior is simple, clear, everyday language. The guidelines developed for use in the Crawford slip method, a large-group tool for sharing and combining knowledge on a topic area, provide useful guidance for structuring narrative data. The guidelines stipulate that each data item be recorded on a separate slip and written in simple terms using short sentences with no acronyms or jargon.

Facts that people already know or can confirm independently are the most persuasive of all arguments. Facts can speak to us in a way that opinions never can. It is as if the mind validates facts and immediately deposits them into our memory bank for use like a cash deposit into a bank. People's opinions, however, are held like a suspect check pending clearance, a transaction that may never occur if our brain becomes distracted.

In contrast, facts put into our active memory energize our thinking, and as we accumulate a number of these facts we start to piece them together into a "whole," like decoding a secret message.

PREVENT MISLEADING OURSELVES AND OTHERS WITH DATA

This insistence on the need to expose people to rich data is echoed by Yale professor Edward R. Tufte, the guru of data displays and visual interpretation.

Tufte criticizes the vogue of using slideshows for all discussions in organizations, the one having a standard font and only a couple of bullet points per slide. He claims that these not only put people's brains to sleep and are not conducive to thinking and discussion, but also are fashioned on the model of a sales pitch. Such overheads clearly appeal to the conscious mind, simple "take-home messages."

Tufte encourages organizations to produce rich, multidimensional displays that provide the subconscious mind with both context and stimulation. Bad graphics, claims Tufte, fail because they omit or manipulate context, deceive by discouraging comparison, obscure important details, and confuse with visual miscues.

Tufte's principles for data display summarize the important issues of data analysis. He advocates that displays of data should always:

- Tell the truth.

- Show the data in its full complexity.

- Reveal what is hidden.

- Respect the receiver.

Just like painting a picture, it helps to keep all the data on a single surface so that the brain can study all the variables simultaneously. In order to allow for group participation, this surface should be visible, such as a flipchart page, whiteboard, or computer display.

A good example of such a process was given by Jerry Hirshberg, who described how he and his auto designers evaluated the system behavior of the Nissan minivan and its owner:

> Scores of owners were invited to Nissan Design Institute with their vehicles, which they were asked to bring in whatever state of tidiness or disarray they were in. We spoke with them openly, directly with no one-way mirrors or hidden cameras. No lengthy questionnaires or surveys. Instead there was much animated talk about how each owner interacted with their vehicles, what worked well, what didn't. And we went for rides with them, anything to tease out (data on) hidden problems or opportunities. Much of this valuable input would not have been thought worth mentioning by the participants, let alone asked about on any marketing questionnaire. On completion of our searches we compiled our varied riches, such as snapshots, scribbled memorable quotes, sketches of ingenious ways people had solved problems. These were exhibited in a large observational collage. This was true research-neutral, unbiased and inquisitive. There was no pressure for immediate demonstrable results. The real value would be ascertained later from the improvements to the product that resulted.

SEPARATE THE CRUCIAL FACTS BY DEVELOPING A STORYLINE OR TWO

When it comes to analyzing data and betting big on the conclusions there are few more widely respected practitioners than Warren Buffet, the world's most famous investor.

The legendary CEO of Berkshire Hathaway has an unrivalled record in earnings growth, over 15 percent per year, maintained over a decade. These earnings derived solely from the skills of Buffet and his deputy chairman, Charlie Munger, in deciding which stocks and which companies to buy.

According to author Janet Lowe, Buffet does not disclose which companies he invests in unless required to by the Securities and Exchange Commission, but he freely explains the principles he uses, which he claims are timeless: "If principles can become dated they're not principles."

His advice is that the key is to understand what you're looking at and what makes it tick. He once likened his analysis of companies to a journalist reporting a story: "Ask a lot of questions, dig up a lot of facts and at the end of it you'll understand the story."

Part of Buffet's research often involves gathering some data firsthand to check the validity of facts that look good on paper. When he was looking to invest in American Express, he sat at the cash register at his local steakhouse to count the number of people paying with Amex.

He also cautions those seeking to understand a company's situation to keep it simple: "If you have to go through too much detailed investigation then something is wrong." In other words, a top-level analysis should reveal a clear and consistent picture; if it doesn't, that is in itself a cause for concern.

Berkshire Hathaway follows this principle when investigating possible acquisitions. When asked on one occasion by U.S. authorities for their staff papers on a company, executives replied, "There aren't any papers. There aren't any staff."

Once the crucial facts are identified, they must now be viewed as a whole to see what they collectively imply. This is "seeing the implications."

SEEING THE IMPLICATIONS

As Dr. Watson explained, "I had listened with great interest to the statement which Holmes, with characteristic clearness, had laid before me. Though most of the facts were familiar to me, I had not sufficiently appreciated their relative importance, nor their connection to each other."

This describes very well an important lesson that we have learned from the evaluations of systems, which is that there are very few facts in the description that each person had not previously been aware of. What is new is the significance of all the data seen together.

As humans we tend to deal separately with each issue or piece of data that we encounter. Each is explained away in our minds. After we have explained away a number of these pieces of data, we are left with no basis for action, because our conscious mind has given the "OK" to the situation. Nevertheless we are left with an unconscious feeling of unease that we may be missing something.

A pioneer of communication theory, Norbert Wiener, drew attention to the fact that data play a role in informing our unconscious mind rather than our conscious actions: "We do not will the motions of certain muscles and indeed we generally do not know which muscles need to be moved to accomplish a task like picking up a pencil.

Our motion is regulated by some measure of the amount by which the task has not yet been accomplished."

This same point is perfectly illustrated by famed tennis coach Tim Gallwey, who tells a story about a player named Jack who sought Gallwey's help to improve his backhand shot.

Jack, who considered his erratic backhand one of the major problems of his life, came rushing to Gallwey during a lunch hour, exclaiming, "I've always had a terrible backhand. Maybe you can help me." Jack said that five other coaches had told him what his problem was: he took his racket back too high on his backswing.

Gallwey's advice was that Jack should take a closer look at his own swing and so placed him in front of a large window where he could make swings and see his own reflection. Jack was astounded by what he observed—that he really did take his racket too high, above his shoulder, in fact.

Gallwey stated that Jack's exclamation was just reporting the data; there was no hint of judgment in his voice.

In other words, Jack now had data on his swing that his unconscious mind could use, rather than a judgment that his conscious mind would only get upset about. By repeating his swings and observing them in the window, Jack was soon able to keep his racket low quite effortlessly. Jack proclaimed: "That feels entirely different than any backhand I've ever swung."

Again Gallwey was struck by the fact that Jack was again not making a judgment that his swing was "fixed" but merely acknowledging how different it felt, reinforcing muscle memory so that his body would repeat the correct motion.

BUFFET'S PRINCIPLES FOR SEEING THE IMPLICATIONS

Buffet's advice on "seeing implications" is to beware of overreaching your knowledge by spreading yourself too thin and trying to reach too many conclusions or make too many decisions. His argument is that all investment decisions are complex and so require both a level of competence in the relevant area of business, and the individual's full attention, if they are to be made successfully. This applies regardless of whether they involve a small investment or a big investment. He argues that you may as well stay focused on the big decisions that are within your "circle of competence" and make sure you do a good job of making them.

Buffet tells business school classes, "You'd be better off if they gave you a ticket with 20 punches on it (rather than an amount of money), and you used a punch every time you made an investment decision. That way you'd save them for the big decisions."

The ability to sift an ongoing flow of data, separate the crucial facts, and see their implications has been shown to be a vital survival capability in studies of 200- and 300-year-old companies.

A study conducted by Arie De Geus and a team from Shell Oil set out to identify the secrets of longevity as practiced by 200- and 300-year-old companies (in contrast to the average company that survives a mere 20 years). The sample included such companies as DuPont, Mitsui, W. R. Grace, Unilever, Hudson's Bay Company, and Siemens.

Not surprisingly all these companies seemed to be very good at adapting to their environment. As De Geus explains:

> as wars, depressions, technologies and politics surged and ebbed, they always seemed to excel at keeping their feelers out, staying attuned to whatever was going on. For information they sometimes relied on packets carried over vast distances by portage and ship, yet they managed to react in a timely fashion to whatever news they received.

These "survivor" companies seemed to do a good job of seeing the implications of the data they monitored. For De Geus found, "They were very prudent with finances, always ensuring they had resources available to ride out temporary reversals or turbulence in the marketplace and take opportunities that such events created for organizations with confidence and cash in hand."

A good process prompted by a suitable model allows these feelings of unease to surface, to be explored, and to be informed by all the data.

STAKEHOLDERS' INVOLVEMENT

For an illustration of how these factors play out, we look at the story of a project team who had to hold a crucial review in unusually difficult circumstances.

It was 1986 and three members of a bid team from a computer company were traveling to New York to meet with a vice president from a very important customer. The VP had requested the meeting. He was unhappy because the team had indicated that it was about to recommend a "no bid" on a large construction project with a significant impact for the VP's area of responsibility.

At their hotel the night before the meeting, the team tried to figure out how to handle the meeting. The central problems were as follows:

- There would be a number of specialists in attendance from the customer organization, some of whom were likely to be hostile, or at the very least skeptical, about anything the team had to say.

- Each point of information was not in itself conclusive. Each could and probably would be explained away. In the language of the courtroom dramas, the evidence was all circumstantial, not outright grounds for convicting the project as a dud.

- Only the whole case viewed as one body of data could convince open-minded individuals that all was not well with the project.

The difficulty was how to get the case across before people waded in with questions and observations. "We can't expect people to hold off their questions and comments for very long—this is not a courtroom with a judge who can grant counsel leave to speak uninterrupted," said one of the team members.

They estimated that they could ask for five minutes to give an uninterrupted overview of the situation, which could then be discussed piece by piece for as long as necessary. They also assumed that they should be prepared for various pieces of the data to be challenged, and that they should be able to make changes to it in the likely event that people could offer facts that contradicted or changed the picture.

They concluded that what they needed was something visible and concise that could be updated as the group offered significant new information.

What they decided to do was to write the sequence of events and key data on large cards. These could be introduced one at a time and pinned up on a corkboard or stuck on a whiteboard that they were confident would be in the meeting room. They had cards with them because they were used in a brainstorming technique that was typically used with customers to identify requirements for their manufacturing systems. So they wrote out the events and key data points on these cards.

In this case the team separated the crucial facts as they saw them. They were also fully aware that the data would have to be sifted again to verify the crucial facts with the customer's team.

THE DYNAMICS OF THE STAKEHOLDER REVIEW

Next morning they took a taxi to the customer's corporate office block and were ushered into a meeting room. They were joined shortly by the vice president, who greeted them cordially and thanked them for making the trip. He introduced them to three others who had various engineering responsibilities.

They asked for five minutes to review the situation and laid out their case well within that time. They then opened up the floor for questions and discussion. The questions came from every aspect: Why were they doing this? How sure were they of these facts? Hence the sifting began.

The conversation stretched over the two hours allowed. The VP canceled his other appointments in order to stay with the topic, and he invited three or four more people into the session to add their perspective. By this time the case was no longer something the team was trying to sell them. Enough data had been shared by their own group to validate the main points of the situation. Thus the crucial facts were agreed upon.

It was becoming clear that a consensus was emerging about what the outcomes would be if current trends continued. From this dialogue the implications emerged with clarity. These conclusions were not to the VP's liking. He ordered in lunch and the discussion switched to what could be done to get things back on track. These ideas were hashed out over the rest of the afternoon, and over dinner that evening the VP resolved to take action on the specific issues that the meeting had identified.

Despite the best efforts of all those involved, the project could not be saved. The risks remained too high, and the next phase was never approved. Although changes were made to the structure of the project, confidence was severely shaken and could not be restored.

The team did not see this as a big success; after all, they had failed to win a contract, but at least they had averted a potentially disastrous project from getting the go-ahead.

What the team had instinctively done was to stumble upon the principles of Holmes, Tufte, and Buffet. Follow a process: sift the data, separate the crucial facts, and see their implications for the project's purpose.

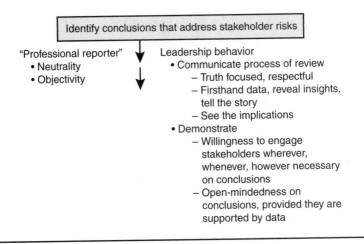

Figure 12.2 Summary of Information step 2.

SUMMARY

The second part of the Information theme concerns the identification of conclusions that address stakeholder risks. It involves:

- Ensuring that the review process follows the commitments made to those who participate.

- Keeping an open mind and encouraging honest sharing of the "real story" so that the facts stay central to the proceedings.

- Facilitating an effective process of analysis that takes account of all relevant data, namely, sifting the data, separating the crucial facts, and seeing the implications. The saying that describes this is, "Facts are stubborn things."

13

Information: Align Stakeholder Decisions

It is one thing to spot a change in the market, or in public attitudes or in the political climate. It is quite another to quickly devise a completely different approach, (perhaps) abandoning an idea to which (the) leader has been passionately committed.
The Economist, Survey of Corporate Leadership, October 2003

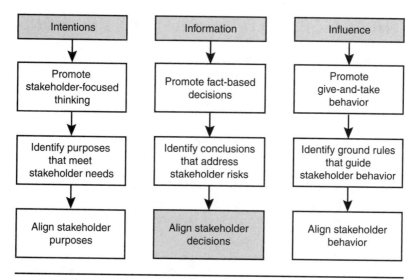

Figure 13.1   Leadership model: Information step 3.

GETTING DIFFICULT DECISIONS MADE

The focus for the leader in the third step of the review is to get collective decisions made. The main difficulty is that people are often reluctant to make difficult decisions that are aimed at avoiding an unwanted outcome that is not yet fully apparent to everyone in the organization. Everyone dislikes having to make changes, and to voluntarily decide to make changes can seem perverse unless the decision maker genuinely believes that failure will be the almost inevitable outcome of inaction. Furthermore the decision maker knows that he or she will have to convince everyone else in the project and perhaps the organization at large of this logic. This gives rise to a fear of conflict. At the heart of the ability to overcome this is the belief that risk factors do not appear from nowhere at a critical level; they first appear as small matters long before and can be detected and acted on while they are still manageable.

As the saying goes: "Coming events cast their shadows before." Identifying the telltale signs that a plan or system is going off track, and acting on them, decisively reduces risks and avoids waste.

THREE STEPS TO DRIVE DIFFICULT DECISIONS

What makes people decide to act is the realization that the conclusions contain information on risks. Risks that are already a problem in their own right could easily combine to create so much damage that the project would go out of control, and stakeholders would likely pull the plug. How does the leader get the participants to see the risks, and to see their imminent potential to interact with unwanted consequences?

Sir John Harvey-Jones's philosophy as expressed in *The Troubleshooter* television series contains three steps for making difficult decisions. Step 1: face up to the worst that could happen. Step 2: look calmly at the difficult choices open to you that will ensure survival/success. Step 3: make a decision in light of the urgent risks of organizational failure you face.

Why these three steps?

Facing up to the worst that could happen forces people to take their head out of the sand and stop denying that organizational failure is not only possible but may in fact be highly probable. The fear of organizational failure will, Sir John hopes, outweigh any lingering desire on the part of decision makers to hang on a little longer in the hope that events will prove their past decisions to have been right all along. The second step addresses the need to follow a structured decision process using all available data and not to succumb to, or

communicate, panic. The third step is to keep a sense of urgency—
not to dither or delay in executing drastic changes if these are called
for—because every delay increases the risk of failure.

In the best of all worlds, we would have objective assessments of
all our risks, but in many cases we do not. This should not stop us
doing the best job we can of assessing them. As experienced mine
manager Garold Spindler explained in putting forward a case for the
need to apply total quality management principles to the management process itself.

> We must continually address risks and plan contingencies.
> Unforeseen events must be considered and probabilities as-
> signed. While this may seem too subjective to be part of a
> well-ordered management process, the consensus of experi-
> enced people is often all that is required.

For an insight into how this three-step process takes place, we
can look at the circumstances that arise in an outdoor expedition,
where risks and adverse outcomes are all too visible.

HOW OUTDOOR GUIDES GET PEOPLE TO MAKE DIFFICULT DECISIONS

Outdoor expedition expert Keith Morton wrote in *Explore Magazine:*

> Significant mishaps [in the outdoors] are not usually caused
> by a single sudden, major occurrence. On the contrary they
> are often the almost inevitable results of a series of acts,
> omissions or minor occurrences. As the trip progresses a
> number of small potential problems can accumulate, eroding
> the safety margin until another, in itself minor problem, puts
> you over the edge.

Morton likened the situation facing an expedition that encounters such a series of problems as accumulating "lemons" as in the
old-style slot machines. Nothing noticeable happens when you accumulate one or two, but when you have a line of them bells ring and
things start happening. An example, says Morton, of such lemon
events for a group of hikers could be:

- It's fall and the days are short.

- They made a late start.

- The group makes a navigation error that takes them off
  course and lengthens their trip.

- The weather deteriorates, rain falls, and the trail becomes slippery.
- One member forgot rain pants and so is soaked, cold, and uncomfortable.

At this point, although the group has not noticed any sudden change in its circumstances requiring a change of plan, they have in fact eroded their safety margin. Morton's advice for the hypothetical hikers mirrors closely Sir John's three steps, namely:

- Face up to the worst that could happen. Morton writes, "Because they are behind schedule and hungry, and need to return to base before dark, they could easily start to hurry and then somebody could slip and twist a knee. Jackpot." The team would now be in a serious predicament and would require external rescue resources to extract them.

- Look calmly at the choices. Morton explains: "They have to re-assess their whole situation, not just look at the problem that triggered the re-assessment. They need to factor in the short length of daylight remaining, the wet and cold team-member who may suffer exposure, etc. This would involve making an inventory of all the assets, equipment and skills at the disposal of the group."

- Make and implement your decision. Delay in the outdoors can be fatal, as changing conditions create new risks.

The leader has a vital responsibility to see that this occurs. When no one has this responsibility or chooses to duck it, failure is never far away. An example of such a situation is the case of the trans-Alaska pipeline project and the subsequent environmental disaster arising from the grounding of the oil tanker *Exxon Valdez*.

HOW A REVIEW COULD HAVE PREVENTED THE EXXON VALDEZ ENVIRONMENTAL DISASTER

The environmental disaster that occurred in 1989 when the *Exxon Valdez* ran aground in Prince William Sound in Alaska is a typical example.

The shadows were cast long before the event itself. To see this we need to look at the inception of the Alaska oil pipeline. Our analysis of this episode relies heavily on the research of author Neil Schlager.

The pipeline runs from the oilfields on Alaska's North Slope to the port of Valdez, where tankers load the crude oil and transport it to refineries elsewhere, such as California.

When the pipeline was first proposed in the 1970s there was much opposition to it from citizens and environmental groups, who claimed that a disaster was almost inevitable with so much tanker traffic in an area with extensive ice flows and rocky coastline.

In order to gain approval for the project, the federal government and oil industry made a number of promises. The key ones were that:

- Ice conditions in Prince William Sound would be carefully monitored with state-of-the-art equipment to minimize the chance of a tanker colliding with ice.

- Tankers would be of the double-hull design, which would greatly reduce oil spillage in the event of a soft collision.

- Safety standards for ship operation, including crew numbers, were stipulated.

- The Valdez Coast Guard station would inspect tankers before they left the terminal. This station would also monitor tankers, using powerful radar as far as Bligh Reef, in order to give warning should they sail too close to the reef.

On the basis of these undertakings, the pipeline was approved in 1974. The implicit purpose of all these undertakings was "to take all possible precautions to avoid oil spills altogether and minimize them should they occur."

Schlager writes: "On the morning of March 23, 1989, the *Exxon Valdez* ran aground on the reef, spilling 10.8 million gallons of crude oil into Prince William Sound." This resulted in more than 1500 miles of shoreline being polluted and many thousands of birds, fish, and sea otters being killed.

The ship had been filled at Valdez and set sail on a routine voyage to California. Sea conditions were difficult because of ice floes, but not exceptional for those waters at that time of year. On the bridge during the crash was a third mate not licensed to pilot in these channels. Although he had received some general instructions from the captain, he was not given a specific course.

He missed seeing the Busby Island light, which was his marker to start the turn right into the channel. Schlager's account describes the final steps in the series of mishaps that led the ship onto the rocks. "On seeing the buoy marking the reef the lookout gave the alarm and the third mate tried to initiate an emergency turn, but the ship would not respond because it was on auto-pilot. The *Valdez* crashed aground on Bligh reef, tearing open its bottom and spewing oil into the surrounding waters."

The response to the spill was slow and confused. Containment equipment was slow to reach the scene and even then did not function as expected.

The inquiry into the disaster showed that none of the promises made before the pipeline was built were in place. All had been shelved because of an economic downturn. In particular:

- Double hulls had not been implemented.

- The spill readiness team members were reassigned to other duties.

- The Coast Guard station had its powerful radar replaced by one less powerful that was incapable of tracking all the way to the reef.

- Manning levels on tankers declined, from 40 crew members in 1977 on the *Valdez* to about 20 in 1989, with consequent long working hours and watch responsibilities falling on inexperienced people.

In other words, the purpose, as demonstrated by actions, was "to take precautions that are affordable right now with the current price of oil."

A review, following the leadership principles outlined in this book, of the status of the operation of tanker traffic through Prince William Sound against the purpose associated with the pipeline's approval could have highlighted the significant departures and prompted action to address them.

GETTING ALIGNMENT ON DECISIONS WITH EACH STAKEHOLDER GROUP

As the "New York project" example showed in Chapter 12, the process of reviewing the data to formulate conclusions may need to be repeated with each stakeholder group in order to generate commitment to act. Also the type of decisions and actions that each stakeholder group takes is likely to be different in keeping with their different circumstances and roles in the issues.

One case that illustrates this process concerns Florence Nightingale (1820-1910), who achieved fame for her leadership of a group of British nurses during the Crimean War during the 1850s.

After the war she dedicated herself to promoting public health. Working with Dr. Farr, a pioneer in public health, Florence, who was a gifted mathematician, analyzed the mortality data from the war, looking for causes that could improve public health policies and military and civilian practices.

What Farr and Nightingale discovered by comparing mortality rates at different hospitals and time periods shocked Nightingale. It emerged that her hospitals at Scutari, which she had enthusiastically expanded and which consequently became overcrowded, had far greater mortality rates than the other hospitals in the region. Further analysis showed that the likely cause was bad hygiene, overcrowding, bad air, and cross infection. In short, all the hygiene issues that are nowadays a central part of modern medical practice but were unknown in the mid-19th century.

Nightingale came to a difficult realization. First, she had inadvertently created conditions in which soldiers had died needlessly because of her ignorance of hygiene. Second, this knowledge had far-reaching implications for public health and must be made available to those with authority and interest in public health.

Farr stated, "Had the conclusions which Florence Nightingale reached been heeded in the civil war in America, hundreds of thousands of lives might have been saved." They were not heeded for the simple reason that they were not published. That missing information, coincidentally, cost the life of Farr's own son Frederick, a Union soldier who died in the final days of the war of a fever caught in an army hospital.

Why were Nightingale's conclusions not published?

What Nightingale wanted, and lobbied for, was a full inquiry into the Crimean campaign, where her findings could be published. Although the inquiry did eventually take place, her data and conclusion were not documented in the final report because there was a power struggle between the government and Queen Victoria over who should command the army. Consequently neither side wanted these findings made public, the queen because she wanted to keep control of the army, the government because the resulting unpopularity might sweep it from office.

Nightingale, a strong-willed and resourceful woman, realized that the inquiry would not do the job and set out to achieve the necessary ends by different means.

The key stakeholders who needed to be informed were civilian and army doctors, those in charge of hospitals and other public health facilities, and the general public, who took the consequences of poor public health policy.

To reach the medical profession and public health policy makers, she created her own distribution list of influential people and sent a copy of her report to each person. The covering letter urged the recipient to act on the information but not to circulate the report or divulge its existence. Historians speculate that this was part of an agreement with the British government, which suppressed publication of the report in the United States, lest it get back to the public in Britain.

To reach the public Nightingale commissioned a journalist to write a history book, *England and Her Soldiers,* into which the findings on public health were to appear without mentioning where they came from. The book was written and priced to appeal to a wide audience. Nightingale's involvement in the project was kept secret and the book's description of her role in the Crimea was of a participant in the system, doing what she could for injured soldiers.

The book sold well and certainly heightened awareness of public health issues, as did the confidential reports. Over time the importance of hygiene was included in the body of standard medical knowledge.

Nightingale's strategy for making sure stakeholders became aware of the risks to health of poor hygiene and how to reduce the risks worked. In fact, historians typically conclude that her work was widely adopted because it had been published. It is a tribute to her leadership.

Is this an isolated example? We believe that situations in which powerful stakeholders do not wish findings to be published freely to all other stakeholders are quite common. That is especially true when the information could change the balance of power.

What Nightingale's example shows is that rather than give way to cynicism, a resourceful leader finds alternative ways to bring about corrective action. This leader uses creativity to communicate conclusions to stakeholders and negotiates with the more powerful stakeholders to ensure that alternative communication channels are not blocked.

These negotiations, involving give and take, are a vital component of the leader's ability to accomplish his or her aims. Rather than dwelling on a sense of disappointment that their "idols" have feet of clay, a leader keeps in mind that those in power, while they may be no better than the average person, may be no worse either. And the average person, Norbert Wiener advised in *Cybernetics,* should never be underestimated. "No (one) is either all fool or all knave. The average (person) is quite reasonably intelligent concerning subjects which come to (their) direct attention and quite reasonably altruistic in matters of public benefit or private suffering which are brought before (their) own eyes."

Enlist the stakeholders' help as individuals to do the right thing, even if they feel unable to use their position directly to do so. Nightingale's approach shows that a resourceful and determined leader can get stakeholders to address critical risks, but that there is seldom a single, easy route to do this.

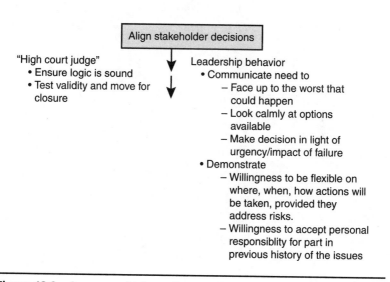

Figure 13.2 Summary of Information step 3.

SUMMARY

The third and final part of the Information theme is aligning stakeholder decisions. It involves:

- Following through from the analysis of data and conclusions to maintain momentum for action by emphasizing the urgency. There is no time for deferring or delaying action, because things cannot get better of their own accord.

- Ensuring that people accept the idea that although dangerous risks are already in play, there are still options.

The saying that describes this is, "Coming events cast their shadows before."

- Facing up to the worst that could happen. Look calmly at the options available, make a decision, and implement it with a sense of urgency.

14

Case Study of a Business That Got Back on Track

There is no better way to improve an organization's performance than to measure the results of (resource) appropriations against the promises and expectations that led to their authorization.

Peter Drucker

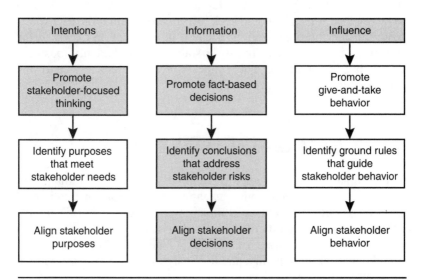

Figure 14.1   Leadership model: Getting a company back on track.

For an example of how to implement Sir John Harvey-Jones's maxims, we can look at one of his cases in *The Troubleshooter* television series. This dealt with the old established family firm of Letts.

When Sir John visited Letts, he found a company in severe financial difficulties. The company had been founded by John Letts, who produced the world's first printed diary in 1812. It sold primarily to business people like the city of London merchants who liked being able to record future events. They also used the information section at the front of the diary for such things as tide tables in order to know when their ships could be expected to arrive and depart the port of London.

The first step was to sift the data and separate the crucial facts.

The typical format was that Sir John would meet with the head of the organization, either the CEO or chairman depending on the nature of the organization. The CEO would provide his or her view of the main difficulties and highlight specific areas where advice was wanted.

Sir John would then have one-on-one meetings with key individuals, usually managers from different areas of the organization, and visit key locations. He would seek information from industry experts from outside the organization, because he was not an expert in the industries himself but primarily a source of fundamental business and management advice. This echoes Warren Buffet's advice to stay within your circle of competence.

DATA ON THE LETTS COMPANY

The company was still owned by members of the Letts family, several of whom occupied senior management positions at the time of Sir John's visit. Although the company was one of the world's largest producers of high-quality diaries, it had diversified into other areas to offset the cyclical nature of the diary business, capitalize on the brand name for high quality, and use spare manufacturing capacity at its Scottish plant.

From the comments of Sir John as detailed in his book, we can identify Letts's key stakeholders in three main groups. They are capital investors who've entrusted their money to Letts, customer investors who've entrusted their business volume to Letts, and competency inventors who've entrusted their skills and energies to the Letts organization. "Capital" investors were:

- The Letts family, who owned 58 percent of the stock
- A venture capital firm, 3i, which owned 21 percent
- Hambro's bank, which had provided refinancing

"Customer" investors were:

- Retail outlets who purchased Letts diaries and other information books for resale

- Corporate customers (especially in the United States and Japan) who purchased multiple copies of diaries, record books, and certificates as in-house incentives and business gifts for their customers

- Individual customers who purchased or used Letts products such as diaries, books, and high-end luggage from Letts's Mayfair Trunks retail store

"Competency" investors were:

- The management group of the Letts companies
- The employees of the Letts group

Sir John's interviews and research brought to light the following expectations and requirements:

- To keep the company in family ownership
- To survive as a company
- To provide an annual profit of 1 million pounds
- To provide continued employment within the United Kingdom for a Letts workforce

- To be responsive to large retailers' and corporate customers' needs for diaries and custom-printed books in terms of product quality, scheduling of orders, deliveries, and competitive pricing

- To meet user needs for high-quality information books, namely, accuracy of information, pages, strength of binding, pleasing appearance, high-quality materials, finish, and so forth

- To have a solid plan to manage the way forward

These data are summarized in the strategy map (Figure 14.2).

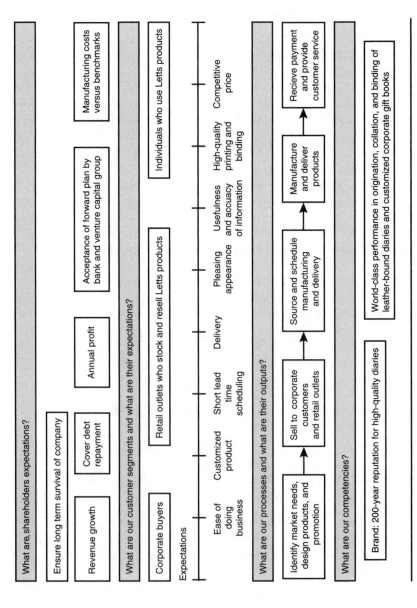

Figure 14.2 Strategy map based on Letts company.

STRATEGY MAPPING

In order to establish a common understanding of the situation, a leader and team need a tool for organizing information, synthesizing views, and prompting thought processes of participants.

In the words of Donald Steward, an expert in large system modeling, the ideal tool acts as "a way of pulling together what a group of people know about a system, to focus and discipline their thinking, while also allowing them to manipulate it to achieve greater insight and a solution."

The strategy map is a relatively new tool, first described in Robert Kaplan and David Norton's book *The Strategy-Focused Organization.* These authors subsequently published a book, *Strategy Maps,* dealing exclusively with strategy maps. It contains a wealth of examples.

They describe a strategy map as "a logical architecture that defines a strategy by specifying the relationships among shareholders, customers, business processes and competencies."

CONCLUSIONS ON THE LETTS COMPANY

In order to identify the shadows that could bring about company failure, Sir John analyzed the actions, decisions, and outcomes of the previous few years. This, he hoped, would provide a clear picture of the issues to the Letts family so that they could take necessary action.

These data are summarized in the Letts data table (Table 14.1). He then set about to "separate the crucial facts."

The underlying problem was that Letts, like many family-owned businesses, had borrowed money to keep the organization afloat through difficult times and this was now a millstone around the company's neck. Combined with their operational issues, this threatened to drag Letts underwater. Sir John identified five key conclusions and risks. There was one for each of the four operating divisions—diary manufacturing, diary/gift marketing and sales, book publishing, and retail store—and one concerning the senior management team itself.

The conclusions are summarized in the Letts conclusions table (Table 14.2). These are illustrated as "gaps" on the strategy map (Figure 14.3).

The manufacturing division, while it had unique capabilities, also had high costs, was inflexible to customer needs, and had long lead times. The risk was that the manufacturing division had

Table 14.1 Letts data table.

1800	• Origins in stationery and business diaries • John Letts founds business in London • Produces first printed diary
1964	• Production moved to improve productivity • Moved printing, binding facility from London to Edinburgh • Less restrictive labor practices, lower cost • Distance from London opens communication gap
1980s	• Diversification to offset cyclic diary business • University study recommends book publishing • Revision (study) guides started • Berlitz travel guides franchise obtained • Distribution center in Scotland opened
1990	• Caught off balance by setbacks in midst of growth • Set up books division, full color, long selling life • Acquired Mayfair Trunks, retail luggage outlet • Recession, rise in interest rates, rate of dollar exchange reversal, reversal in Mideast (Arab diaries business lost because of Kuwait War)

1991	• Restructuring to address immediate realities
	• Red alert—bank put company on intensive care list
	• Revision guides sold to raise cash
	• Restructuring of company: three divisions
	   –Book and diary publishing
	   –Printing, binding, distribution
	   –Overseas marketing and distribution of diaries and corporate gifts
	• Refinancing of company—requirement for repayment 1992 onward (£1 million profit)
	• Recovery plan—redundancies, rationalize products

April 1992	• Sir John Harvey-Jones invited to advise on way forward

become "the tail that wagged the dog," a recipe for failure in a competitive market.

The diary/gift marketing division had a promising future, but it was at risk because there was no process for coordination with manufacturing. The other two divisions, book publishing and the retail store, had been started in order to leverage the Letts brand name but neither was contributing to the bottom line or providing any real synergies to the core business.

The book publishing division had a promising future but needed upfront investment. The risk here was that it would either fail through

Table 14.2   Letts conclusions table.

• Scottish facility is the tail that wags the dog
   –Specialist machines, competitive advantage
   –Some highly manual, some out-of-date technology
   –Long lead times (six weeks to produce diary, four-month lead time)
   –Lots of pieces and products
   –Printing operation needs investment

• Letts of London looks like future of core business
   –Potential overseas opportunities (especially the United States and Japan) for diaries and corporate gifts
   –Exploits expertise unique to Letts, world-class small bound diaries, gives access to corporate customers for wider recognition gifts

• Book publishing potential in jeopardy
   –Not yet profitable, needs investment
   –No use of Letts production facility

• Mayfair Trunks an expensive luxury
   –High-quality image, unprofitable
   –Low synergy with diaries, less than 5 percent Letts products

• Management's way forward?
   –Significant gap between production/sales (no link below board)
   –Sense of urgency appears to be missing (tinkering, trade our way out, look for partners)
   –Some focus on cost but insufficient on profit
   –Crossroads for family ownership: sell off or sell out

lack of investment or cause the downfall of the whole company if it received investment that the company could really not afford.

The retail store, Mayfair Trunks, was not profitable and was a poor fit with Letts's core competencies of marketing, publishing, and custom-manufacturing books.

The senior management team, although capable and highly committed, had an insufficient focus on profitability and a lack of urgency about addressing the imminent risks of business failure. The fact that family members headed up some of these divisions, and as part owners could block change, was another barrier and increased the risks.

DECISIONS OF THE LETTS COMPANY

In order to help Letts to make the decision, Sir John had its executives consider the three steps of first facing up to the worst that could

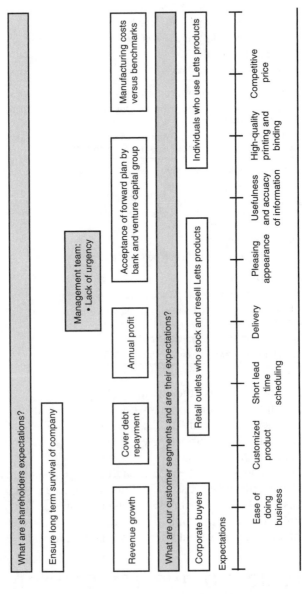

Figure 14.3   Strategy map based on Letts Company showing key issues.

Continued

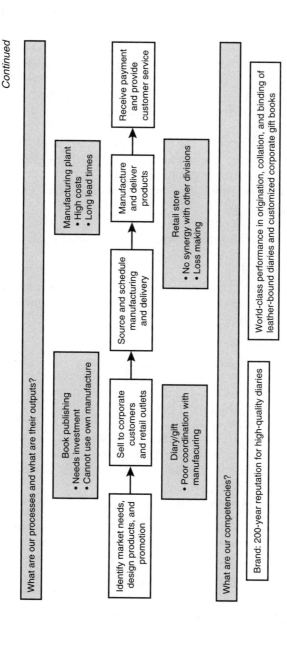

Figure 14.3 Strategy map based on Letts Company showing key issues.

happen. This brought home the necessity of bold action and shook them free of any lingering shreds of denial or vain hopes that things would somehow work themselves out. Second, he got them to look at the options that would address the risks.

The decisions to be made followed directly from these conclusions and risks: sell the book publishing division based on its potential and so raise cash, and sell the retail store to raise cash and reduce operating costs. Streamline manufacturing to improve responsiveness, lower costs, and lead times. Focus attention on the core business and especially in the growing markets in North America and the Far East.

Third, he got them to make a bold decision and implement a plan to address all the risks they faced. The success of this step rested on the work done by Sir John in all the previous steps.

The senior managers of Letts and, crucially, the family board members participated in each of the steps.

Under Sir John's guidance they faced up to the worst that could happen, looked calmly at the difficult choices, and made a decision sufficiently bold to address all major risks.

As a consequence they reluctantly took the decisions that they now realized were vital. Letts of London is still a successful publisher of high-quality diaries, with customers throughout the world, including this author.

SUMMARY

This case study of a real company, based on published information, shows that the leaders of an organization, faced with a very difficult business environment, can use this leadership model to achieve decisive action. In particular the Information theme was executed superbly well, with due attention paid to Intention, and as we shall see later, to Influence.

Highlights of this case were:

- The process of sifting data to separate the crucial facts and to discover the implications; when performed objectively, it leads to clear stakeholder decisions.

- The importance of communication; draw attention to the data and document key points (for example, with a strategy map) and articulate insights.

- The importance of demonstration; clearly show that the stakeholders own their decisions.

15

Influence: Promote Give-and-Take Behavior

Leadership is always dependent on the context, but the context is established by the relationships we value. We cannot hope to influence our situation without respect for the complex network of people who contribute to our organizations.

Margaret Wheatley

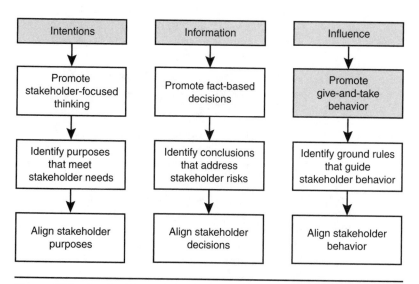

Figure 15.1   Leadership model: Influence step 1.

PERSONAL BEHAVIOR OF LEADER IS CRUCIAL

The main methods that the leader has available to counteract competitiveness are his or her own behavior and personal credibility. The essence of this behavior is the belief that by giving people undivided attention, a skillful leader can influence the environment toward greater cooperation and less competitiveness.

As the old saying goes: "A good beginning makes a good ending." Results are achieved through relationships. Consequently, investments of time to establish and maintain these on a sound basis pay big dividends.

A source of information on the skills that leaders need comes from a study of the behaviors of successful negotiators, who had a track record of gaining more cooperation from people than the average negotiator.

Neil Rackham's research into business negotiations has yielded a list of behaviors that successful negotiators use with a significantly different frequency than average negotiators.

These can be summarized in terms of two sets of composite behaviors, namely, respectfulness and credibility, and transparency and objectivity. I have grouped Rackham's findings under these headings.

TO PROMOTE GIVE-AND-TAKE, TALK LESS ABOUT YOURSELF

Rackham's studies show that successful negotiators "express far fewer positive value statements about themselves (quarter as many), make far fewer defensive or attacking comments (less than a third), make far fewer counterproposals (half as many), and give far fewer reasons for each argument they propose (half as many)."

Displaying respectfulness and credibility is about those behaviors that the effective negotiator uses less often than the average person. This composite behavior is about creating a receptive audience for information and proposals in the other party.

The image that some people have of a good negotiator is some one who "takes control" of the discussion by bombarding their opposite number with attacking comments, boastful remarks, and numerous proposals and counterproposals with plenty of arguments for each. The picture that emerges from Rackham's research shows that effective negotiators do exactly the opposite. They are seen to be in full control of themselves, not attempting to control the other person and not being controlled by them. The last of Rackham's points is very surprising to anyone who learned to make a case at school, where the maxim was the more reasons the better. Rackham explains that in negotiation, advancing weaker arguments provides a soft target for an opponent to attack; once damage is sustained, it creates a psychological disadvantage. The proposal's logic, once punctured, sinks like a ship with a big hole below the waterline.

TO PROMOTE GIVE-AND-TAKE, ASK MORE ABOUT THEM

Transparency and objectivity is about behaviors that the successful negotiator uses much more often than the average negotiator. This composite behavior is about making optimal use of information to create an agreement that is acceptable to both parties.

Rackham found that successful negotiators "used questions to gather information (twice as often) and tested and summarized conclusions (twice as often)." This objectivity gives the negotiators an increased amount of clarified, usable information as a basis for decision making.

The reliability of this information seems to be increased by other transparency behaviors reported by Rackham, namely, "expressed their feelings about the situation and its implications (twice as often) and gave advance notice of what they intended to use (four times as often)."

Studies have shown that transparency is a vital ingredient in customer interactions in which the customer views the service provider as having knowledge and power that they can use either to help the customer's interests or to confuse the customer and take advantage of them. We can argue that the more credible the negotiator, the more important transparency becomes.

It seems no accident that the most significant difference between successful and average negotiators concerns the practice of being courteous and considerate and reassuring the other party by communicating your intentions.

A successful negotiator, like a successful leader, behaves in a way that optimizes the shared analysis of data as a basis of agreement. All distractions should be damped down so that emotional reactions and responses do not sidetrack the decision process of either party.

HOW PERSONALLY PROMOTING GIVE-AND-TAKE WORKS

One way to see how these behaviors lead to success is to use Edward De Bono's "logic bubble" analogy.

A logic bubble is the bubble of perception within which a person is acting. The logic bubble includes both the actual circumstances surrounding a person and also their perception of the situation.

According to De Bono, it is of primary importance when interacting with another person to keep in mind that no matter how illogical their actions and opinions may seem to be from our perspective, the actions and opinions are often completely logical when seen from the other person's perspective. In effect, he says, each of us walks around living in our own logic bubble and consequently, in order to gain mutual understanding, it is vital to exchange information so that each logic bubble can be seen by both parties.

Rackham's identified behaviors can be seen as either showing the other party what's in your own logic bubble or probing the contents of theirs, and avoiding any hostile moves that could cause them to close up like a clam and block your view of their logic bubble.

Respectfulness and credibility create the willingness in the other party to let you see the content of their logic bubble and to be interested in understanding the contents of your logic bubble.

Transparency and objectivity allow you to gently test the contents of their logic bubble and contrast it with your own, thus influencing the other party.

Few better illustrations of these skills can be found than those used by Sir John Harvey-Jones in his activities as the Troubleshooter. Earlier we looked at his visit to Letts and in particular the analysis and decision-making aspects of his task. Here we return to the Letts case to look at the way in which he won the trust of the senior managers and staff at Letts, and built a cooperative working relationship.

PERSONALLY PROMOTING GIVE-AND-TAKE THROUGH RESPECTFULNESS AND CREDIBILITY

A key leadership behavior is expressing few positive value judgements about oneself. Sir John goes one step further by expressing positive value judgements about the contributors he contacted. These were not just generic compliments that could be interpreted as manipulative, but specific, well-researched, positive opinions. He went to great lengths to find out about the contributors' background and qualifications and treated their past efforts and current views with respect. Such phrases as:

"Including a period with Guinness, an excellent alma mater for anyone interested in branding and selling . . ."

"First-class professional with considerable background in finance, he trained at Pricewaterhouse and was a management consultant there . . ."

"Has a firm grip of the risks . . ."

He also attempts wherever possible to find something positive to say about each person.

"I was impressed by the positive attitude . . ."

"Highly realistic and has a natural feel for his business . . ."

"Breathes commitment, drive and enthusiasm, and her team are equally dynamic . . ."

"An extremely nice man . . ."

Because of his success in growing ICI into a world-class organization and because of his down-to-earth personality and excellent communication skills, Harvey-Jones was at the time the best-known British business executive and arguably the most respected.

He positioned himself as a person of experience and an objective seeker after truth, not as someone who had "the answers." His business experience provided him with three precious commodities. First, he could empathize with decision makers because he had been in their shoes and consequently did not underestimate or oversimplify their task. Second, he had experienced firsthand a wide variety of circumstances and therefore could hope to find a similar one from his past that might offer relevant lessons for the situation at hand. Third, it gave him a sense of humility, knowing that despite what the textbooks say, there is never a single "correct" answer to any business problem and consequently the first duty of an advisor is to be constructive and helpful rather than critical and unhelpful.

PERSONALLY PROMOTING GIVE-AND-TAKE THROUGH TRANSPARENCY AND OBJECTIVITY

Another skilled behavior that Sir John employed was transparency. He communicated to the other individual what he was thinking, how he felt, and what he was concerned about. This, as Rackham noted, helps give the other person a sense of security and builds trust. Two things in particular that Sir John did were to give warning of the behavior to be used (for example, saying, "I'd like to ask you a question at this point") and the expression of own feelings ("I can't help feeling worried about the lack of profitability").

Expressing emotions as concerns to bring people's attention to them included these statements:

"If the heralded economic upturn occurred, but I was uneasy . . ."

"I was shocked to find that . . ."

"In my experience, profit does not fall out (by itself), if no one is responsible for it."

"I had a number of smaller concerns . . ."

"The people I (had) talked to so far did not show the urgency which I would have expected."

"I questioned David about the links with the sales team and the flexibility of manufacturing, and he readily agreed that they left something to be desired . . ."

Another key behavior that Sir John exhibited was the ability to gather information by asking questions and checking his understanding by summarizing. The evidence of this is contained in the data tables (Tables 14.1 and 14.2) and charts (Figures 14.2 and 14.3) shown earlier.

This also includes the behavior of making fewer proposals and giving fewer reasons for them.

EXAMPLE OF PROMOTING GIVE-AND-TAKE BEHAVIOR: APOLLO 13

The power of give and take in daily decision making is equally important. Few examples show this better than the way that the critical "lunar burn" decision was made during the Apollo 13 crisis. It involved the leader, deputy director of the Manned Spacecraft Center, Chris Kraft, driving a decision-making process within NASA that took input from hundreds of people and came out with a carefully considered decision within a very short time. This example sheds light on the behaviors that a leader must use to run such decision processes; they echo Rackham's findings from earlier in this chapter.

The situation was an accident in space that had left the three-man crew of Apollo 13 in great danger, traveling toward the moon in a damaged spacecraft. A new flight plan had to be created from scratch. A crucial decision was the timing and length of "burn," or engine thrust, that would send the damaged craft looping around the moon's gravity field and back toward earth.

Astronaut Jim Lovell's book, later made into an acclaimed movie (*Apollo 13*) tells the story of how the decision was made, and Chris Kraft's role in it.

Kraft is considering the decision that must soon be made. His off-duty flight directors, Gerald Griffin and Milt Windler, who lead the operational shift teams in Mission Control, have been polling their team members for ideas and input for several hours, and Kraft is now ready to find out what they've concluded.

"Some people are getting together to discuss all this in the viewing room, and we're going to have to be able to explain things to them as best we can," said Kraft. "Would you be ready to talk about them in an hour?"

Kraft went on, "Before that I want to meet with all the flight directors to make sure we've got our ducks in a line." On reaching a suitable room, Kraft "closed the door, sat, and inclined his head wordlessly to his flight directors inviting them to tell him what they knew." Kraft, according to Lovell's account, "Listened, nodding occasionally but saying nothing. When (they) were done Kraft went to work, raising questions, challenging the estimates, and on the whole trying to anticipate the grilling that would be forthcoming from the VIP room."

Once they had been over all the arguments, Kraft and the flight directors made their way to the meeting room where NASA's senior executives were waiting to hear the options.

Kraft started the briefing by stating the purpose of the meeting. "In about twelve hours, we're going to need to execute our burn. Our objective will be to get the crew home as fast as possible while stretching our consumables as far as possible. The flight directors have come up with some possible burns, and since it's Griffin's team that worked out so many of the numbers, I'll let them explain them."

After outlining the options and the risks of each, Kraft and his team waited for the questions to start. They didn't have long to wait; the merits of the options were analyzed and weighed through a dialogue that crisscrossed all the levels of NASA's hierarchy present in the room.

As the options narrowed through discussion and people started to settle on one, Kraft moved to call the "decision." Instead of "moving a motion" as in more formal settings, he declared the decision and then looked for any signs of lingering doubt or serious objections, on the basis that this group had shown itself fully capable of voicing concerns over any proposal they didn't understand or fully support. When he didn't see any such hesitation, the decision was adopted.

> "So it's agreed, at 70 hours and 27 minutes there will be an 850 foot per second burn for four and half minutes, aiming for a Pacific splash at 142 hours. If all goes well Apollo 13 will be home by Friday afternoon. Everyone in the room nodded, and almost simultaneously, rose and began to move toward the doors."

So the decision was made and everyone then scrambled to get to their stations and start implementation.

Throughout this decision process, Kraft displayed the key behaviors of a leader, as given by Rackham earlier in this chapter.

First, he demonstrated his respectfulness and credibility in a number of ways. He attentively listened without interruption to his flight directors' explanation of the options, knowing like all skilled leaders that nothing concentrates your mind like the full attention of an experienced and astute individual who never lets their own thoughts or words distract them from concentrating on the logic of your argument. Too many senior people get drawn into a premature discussion and thereby release the positive tension that is key to both creativity and accountability. Attentive listening from a credible leader is one of the most powerful forms of recognition anyone can receive. Kraft's credibility was sky high because he had been a flight director for the Gemini program, was well acquainted with the science of spaceflight, and could manage the interface with NASA's top brass. His full attention was the best contribution he could make to preparing his team for the crucial task ahead.

Second, Kraft's transparency played a crucial role in the success of the decision process in arriving at a consensus. He signaled to the flight directors ahead of time what the next moves were:

> "We're going to have to explain things to them as best we can."

> "Would you be ready to talk to them in an hour?"

> ". . . make sure we've got own ducks in a line, let's find a place to talk."

Also, instead of taking up valuable minutes telling the flight directors that he was going to listen to their explanations, he merely gestured that he was already listening, which also communicated eloquently "no time to waste, no words to waste."

His approach to questioning was clearly intended to bring to the surface vital information and judgment on the relative risks of all the options, not merely to help him choose which he thought best. Kraft's objectivity was key to setting the stage for the discussion in the viewing room, the flight director team's task was to "explain things" not to say "here's what we should do," although it is revealed in the story that they had a preferred option as a team. Under Kraft's leadership they did not skew that discussion by pushing one option but "let the arguments play out."

USE OF SYMBOLS IN PROMOTING GIVE-AND-TAKE BEHAVIORS

In relationships that are starting over, a more symbolic and visible sign of the principle of give-and-take is often needed. Such an example is the Wampum Treaty Belt, presented by the First Nations of Canada to the Law Society of Upper Canada, the law college in Ontario. This belt and presentation ceremony was intended to advocate some new ground rules for the relationship between aboriginal communities and peoples and the rest of Canada's society and peoples.

The artwork, known as a two-row Wampum Treaty Belt, was presented to the society in 1998 and is made from beads made from clamshells. The belt has a background of white beads containing two purple rows that run parallel from one end of the belt to the other.

It demonstrates the power of symbols to communicate respect and transparency. An inscription explains its meaning:

> The background of the white beads represents a river and the two parallel rows of purple beads represent two vessels traveling the river. It is recognized that the river is large enough for the two vessels to travel along it together. In one vessel shall be found the Kanien'kehaka (Indian people), and in the other, non-aboriginal peoples.
>
> Each vessel shall carry the laws, traditions, customs, languages and spiritual beliefs of each nation; in short all that makes a people who they are.
>
> It is the responsibility of the people in each vessel to steer a straight course. Neither side shall attempt to bring or force

their laws, traditions, customs, language or spirituality on the people in the other vessel. Such is the agreement of mutual respect that is recorded in the two row Wampum Treaty Belt.

As anyone familiar with Canadian history will know, aboriginal peoples have much experience of their "cultural vessel" being interfered with by nonaboriginal society.

Aboriginal leaders took an opportunity in late 1998 to start relationships afresh with Ontario's legal profession, triggered by a statement earlier that year by the law organization's treasurer vowing to "recognize and respect the uniqueness and richness of aboriginal cultures and nations."

It is a testimony to the ability of people to make a fresh start on their relationships.

WHEN GIVE-AND-TAKE CAN SUCCEED AND WHEN IT CANNOT

In combating the primary barrier of internal competitiveness, the crucial behavior is that of cooperation, in particular the implementation of the principle that "give and take is fair play." In order to identify what the leader needs to do, it is worthwhile understanding how an environment characterized by competition (never give a sucker an even break) can evolve into one characterized by cooperation.

Returning to our discussion of "compete" or "cooperate" decisions, we are not doomed to undermine each other indefinitely. There is hope. If we assume people's dealings are repeated—in other words, we do encounter the other player again and they have some sanctions available to use against us—the success strategies can change dramatically.

What we want to explore here is the notion that relationships between people within organizations can be summarized by their personal strategies relative to one another. These in turn influence and are influenced by the relative frequency of each of the types of personal strategy existing in the organization.

The issue of how well different personal strategies work when pitted against one another in repeated contests has been explored in a large-scale computer simulation by political scientist Robert Axelrod. Richard Dawkins (in *The Selfish Gene*) describes how Axelrod invited experts in game theory to submit strategies, and he played them off against one another in a long series of prisoners' dilemma encounters.

The winning strategy turned out to be "Tit-for-Tat," submitted by Professor Anatol Rappoport of Toronto. Tit-for-Tat begins by cooperating on the first move and thereafter simply copies the previous move of the other player. Tit-for-Tat came out top in five out of six rounds of competition.

What this showed was that Tit-for-Tat, a nice but provocable strategy, could hold its own against nastier ones in the long run.

This is a profound conclusion. In effect, a "fair minded person with backbone" can always prevail over a self-serving person, provided that the environment is not dominated by self-serving, competitive people. In such a case, the sheer number of self-serving individuals that any individual will encounter is likely to overwhelm them, unless they can buffer themselves by surrounding themselves with like-minded people or forming a supportive network.

Axelrod found that in a culture that has come to be dominated by "always compete," no other strategy can do better. This brings to mind some monopolistic organizations that one encounters daily that seem to bristle with internal competitiveness and seem stuck in this mode no matter how many millions of dollars they spend on "change programs."

Furthermore, he found that in a culture that is not completely dominated by "always compete" it is quite possible to have a culture with Tit-for-Tat dominant in one area and "always compete" in another area. It is then a matter of luck which one then comes to dominate. This helps explain what many observers of organizational behavior have commented on, that organizations are made up of many subcultures.

This validates Stephen Covey's habit of "think win-win." Covey points out that win-win cannot survive in a hostile environment. Mutually beneficial, lasting solutions are achieved by people with a win-win frame of mind who work through a win-win process in an environment governed by win-win systems.

The implications for leaders who seek to operate on a basis of give-and-take is that it is essential to assess the environment carefully and regularly. If the environment is shifting toward "always compete," pick your battles carefully.

Using give-and-take in low-risk areas could act as a diagnostic to give an assessment of whether people are using "always compete" or "go-and-take" because they don't want to be treated like a sucker or, alternatively, because they believe most others to be suckers and want to take advantage of them. If they are mostly scared of being taken advantage of, then gradual introduction of give-and-take will build trust to the extent that it forms a subculture. From there it can become self-reinforcing.

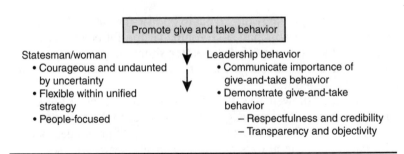

Figure 15.2   Summary of Influence step 1.

SUMMARY

The first part of the Influence theme concerns the leader promoting give-and-take behavior, mainly through personal action, involving:

- Making a commitment to spend personal time and effort in collaboration with people. The saying that describes this is, "A good beginning makes a good ending."

- Less is more. To build trust, be more focused on what the other party has to say, ask many questions, express personal feelings, and state needs and proposals succinctly.

- Use their data. To build a solution, synthesize the information gathered from them with data already shared. Summarize and replay it to them, and think out loud.

16

Influence: Identify Ground Rules That Guide Behavior

I believe that if you are an optimist then you have a chance of creating a self-fulfilling prophecy.

Arthur C. Clarke, scientist, futurist and author
(of such works as *2001: A Space Odyssey*)

I replied that the Atlantic Charter was not a law but a star.

Winston Churchill, about the principles he and
Franklin D. Roosevelt wrote in 1941 to define the Allies' stand

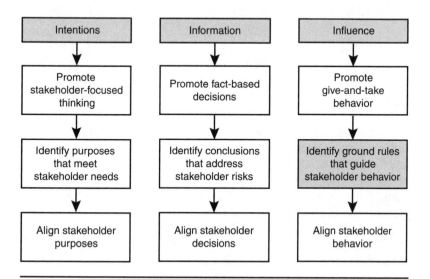

Figure 16.1   Leadership model: Influence step 2.

THE NEED FOR GROUND RULES FOR BEHAVIOR

The danger within a tit-for-tat culture surrounded by a culture of "always compete" is that people can become wary of "starting a war" and therefore abstain from engaging in any action that might be interpreted as aggressive, such as questioning a business proposal that the "other side" is supporting. In such cases it is of paramount importance to explain the action, either as a mistake or as in support of a higher-order goal shared by both sides.

This means that if a give-and-take environment is to survive amid highly competitive cultures, implicit and explicit ground rules need to be developed to help people avoid falling into combative behavior by accident. Once competitiveness has broken out, it will quickly take hold and cannot be reversed.

One such incident in World War I was researched by Axelrod (and quoted by Dawkins).

> Suddenly a salvo of (shells) arrived but did no damage. Naturally both sides got down and our men started swearing at the Germans, when all at once a brave German got onto his parapet and shouted out—"We are very sorry about that; we hope no-one was hurt. It is not our fault, it is that damned Prussian artillery.

Presumably the German officer felt compelled to take such a risk because of what he and his comrades stood to lose if the British forces, with whom he had an unofficial truce, interpreted the shelling as a resumption of local hostilities.

The lessons that we can draw from this analysis are that to create and maintain cooperative working relationships, the following ground rules are crucial: Any action that could be interpreted as "taking advantage" must be carefully communicated, preferably before it starts, but in worst case explained immediately afterward before it provokes a negative response. Anyone on the receiving end of such an action should pause and seek an explanation before responding.

The saying that describes this is "Give-and-take is fair play." Agreements that survive adversity are based on each person getting something they need and foregoing something they wanted.

As Stephen Covey points out in his Habit 2: Begin with the end in mind. For our daily actions to contribute to our long-term vision, we need to translate the vision into practical principles that can guide action. There is no more crucial area for practical principles than behavioral ground rules.

GROUND RULES CAN TAKE MANY FORMS

What do such ground rules look like? They can take many forms, such as a list of operating principles to which a group holds themselves accountable, or they can be embedded in the work structure and process. Ideally they are incorporated into all of these in a consistent way.

The informal ground rules used by winning teams in the world's toughest race provide another example. The Discovery Channel's Eco-Challenge endurance race typically takes seven days to complete. A casual observer might be forgiven for assuming that team members' relationships with one another would be stressed and at the breaking point during the 80 hours of the race. For most teams, and certainly for the winning teams, this is not so, and it appeared to be a critical reason why they were winning teams.

In 1997, journalist Tom Mueller interviewed teams during the race. His conclusions were surprising. What he showed was not the image of success that TV shows typically portray or that highly paid sports teams exhibit. There was no strutting or posturing, no temper tantrums. He found that the winning teams had deep commitment to give-and-take that was further fueled by their achievements.

Said one member of a leading team, "Whenever a tough decision has to be made, we all confer on it. Conflicts are brought out in the open and resolved as a team. We never resort to the 'one ultimate leader' paradigm." Another said, "We're here to learn and enjoy, and will never sacrifice our friendship for a competition."

In another example, ground rules appear as resource allocation principles.

In the Canadian province of Ontario, community care services provided by the provincial health organization are administered by Community Care Access Centers (CCACs). These organizations identify community needs, develop services, contract with service providers, and monitor individual needs and services provided.

In 2001 a CCAC was faced with a sudden budget crisis three months into the fiscal year. It was required to bring a projected $3.5 million deficit into line. The management team set out formal principles of give-and-take that defined how relationships with each of its stakeholders should be conducted:

- Cost containment strategies and reasons for these strategies will be communicated to clients, service providers, public, and institutions.

- Cost containment strategies that are put in place will be those that have the lowest risk to clients.

- The infrastructure will be preserved to support clients and to link them with other available community services.

- We will support staff throughout the cost containment measures. It is recognized that this is a stressful time for all clients, public, and staff.

- We will work with service providers to minimize the impact on their agencies.

- All our branches will be impacted fairly.

The implementation of these principles proved far from straightforward, and the fact that principles were defined did not change the fact that the funding cuts adversely impacted stakeholders. However the management team's review of what subsequently happened, in light of the principles, enabled specific changes to be identified and lessons to be learned much more rapidly. The CCAC continues to be a fast learner and is recognized as a leader among its peers.

CREATING GROUND RULES FOR GIVE-AND-TAKE: A SALES AND SERVICE TEAM

A group of sales and service people based in Europe, working for a large computer company, looked to improve their results in a tough market.

This team was struggling to cope in a new environment. The company's shift of focus toward services and away from product lines, combined with an exhortation to "team sell," was causing massive confusion. Previous relationships based on an individual salesperson making a request to a service specialist for one isolated issue changed to a need for integrated plans and coordinated execution of plans. As one senior salesperson said, "As a salesperson I am told that I am 'empowered' but seem to have more people than ever to negotiate with."

This team decided to talk through its situation and define how to cope. This involved understanding stakeholders, their needs, and a purpose. Also, they needed to identify core work that delivered against this purpose and essential support work needed to sustain their capability to deliver.

The team identified the core work and support work and defined responsibilities for each part of it. This is illustrated in the strategy map (Figure 16.2).

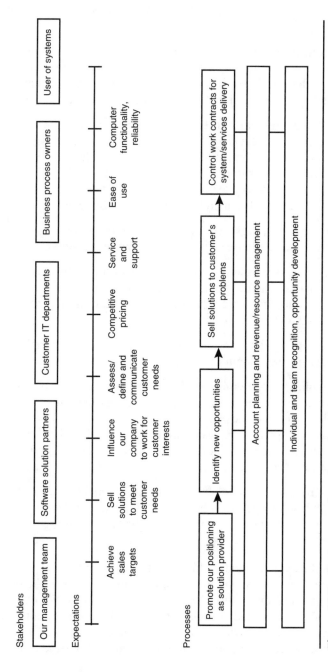

Figure 16.2   Strategy map for sales and service team.

As a result of their discussions, the team defined the following key ground rules in relation to crucial aspects of how the core business process should operate:

Account planning: Account owner to define the ongoing dialogue they want the customer's senior management to have with us and identify which of our senior managers are needed to assist us. Plan how to use them as resources.

Solution selling capability: Every team member should have a declared service/solution selling specialty, for which they monitor the company's capability and update the rest of the team (for example, intelligent building, desktop services). In this way team members can act as specialist salespeople for other members of the team on request.

Customer meetings: After customer meetings, key information should be communicated within the team.

- Call reports should be written whenever there are actions on anyone who did not attend the meeting or when information has arisen that has obvious impact on other's projects with the customer.

- "Interesting" background information should be shared at "open-forum" donut meetings.

Controlling work contacts: Everyone should develop their own contacts in the technical service centers that they use regularly because these personal relationships work best. For centers likely to be used infrequently, go through Bob, who will manage our interface with them, negotiate, and make sure "yes" means "yes."

Recognition: All members of team should make visible recognition of work well done, both that by other team members and that by people outside the team working on its behalf.

Thus the team defined within each ground rule the intention, the influence of each party, and the key information to be used/reviewed in each of the difficult parts of their core process steps. For example, the salesperson who had complained of having too many interfaces to manage now had clarity on what those interfaces were and how they should be managed, both within the team and outside it.

ALIGNMENT OF GOALS AND RECOGNITION

Like many organizations, they had different recognition and reward schemes for each function, and the team members belonged to four functional groups. The criteria for these and the nature and scale of the awards were quite different. In particular the sales awards involved bonuses and vacations, while the service awards involved coffee mugs. This was a small crack in their unity. The real recognition, the recognition that counted, however, came from within the team itself, rather than from outside. Team members knew how hard the goals were to achieve, and team celebrations marked major accomplishments such as the signing of a major systems contract or high customer satisfaction survey scores.

Because of their work on team purpose, ground rules, and roles, the district office, regional HQ, and all functional managers knew about the team and its goals. As a result, individual team members' objectives, as agreed with their functional managers, aligned very well with the team's plan. Consequently, performance reviews for team members were based on data coming from account team reviews and business reporting. These discussions focused on individual development. Again, the most important source for development opportunities was the team itself, where a colleague could include someone on a task for experience and give coaching if needed.

The team went on in the subsequent two years to exceed their sales revenue targets by a significant amount. The team never resolved the reward issues but worked around them. For instance, the senior salesperson won a Mediterranean cruise as a reward for his record sales performance. Believing that the team actually achieved the result, not he alone, he declined the trip. He did not tell the team this until some time after, and although no one said anything it proved a watershed event. The rewards issue was never mentioned again.

Identify ground rules that guide stakeholder behavior

"Broadway producer/promoter"
 • Enthusiasm to make things
   happen
 • Seach for benefits for
   stakeholders
 • Soundly based optimism

Leadership behavior
 • Communicate
   – The importance of selecting
     carefully where to invest time
     in relationship building
     and why
   – The need to identify ground
     rules for give and take
     between stakeholders on
     specific matters of concern
 • Demonstration
   – Build ground rules into
     systems/structures

Figure 16.3   Summary of Influence step 2.

SUMMARY

The second part of the Influence theme concerns the identification of ground rules that guide stakeholder behavior. This involves:

- Identifying issues where expectations need to be established among stakeholders and leading a discussion to arrive at guidelines based on give-and-take, that is, either formally documented or informally adapted into the culture.

- Maintaining two-way communication and creating a win-win situation. An agreement that provides mutual benefit. The saying that describes this is "Give-and-take is fair play."

17

Influence: Align Stakeholder Behavior

An ethic can be seen, not in abstraction, but in behavior. On the Day of Judgment, you will not be asked if you are Christian, Muslim, Buddhist or Hindu; but will be asked "What have you done?"
UNESCO Universal Ethics Conference 1998

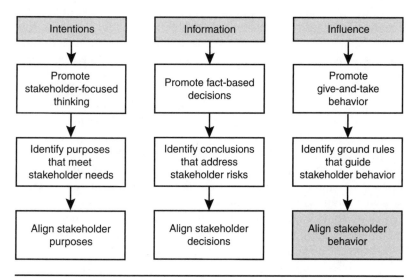

Figure 17.1   Leadership model: Influence step 3.

MODELING AND MONITORING THE BEHAVIOR DESCRIBED IN THE GROUND RULES

In order for give-and-take to survive in the short term, everyone must be continually reminded of two things. First, the ability and willingness to penalize aggressive self-serving behavior exists. Second, individuals or subgroups can never "win" if this is at the expense of the rest of the organization. The key actions of a leader in helping create this environment are to set and communicate these ground rules, preferably in a collaborative way, then to ensure that they become ingrained in the culture of the organization through the credibility of the results. Credibility will keep people's behavior centered on give-and-take for mutual benefit.

As the saying goes, "Nothing succeeds like success." A successful venture must first gain the support of credible people and then retain their support through regular delivery of valued outcomes.

The two behaviors that leaders use here are modeling and monitoring the ground rules. Modeling means that most importantly the leader must ensure that his or her own actions are in line with the ground rules. A leader who is seen to break the rules renders them worthless and creates more cynicism than if the rules had not been defined in the first place.

Monitoring involves the leader in holding everyone accountable for their behavior relative to the ground rules. This involves recognizing and rewarding appropriate behavior and holding nonperformers accountable. This is mostly about noticing, drawing people's attention to their behavior, and asking for an explanation. In this regard it is crucial for the leader to have at their disposal, and for people to know about, several sanctions that can be used if self-serving behavior should start within the project. A leader who always seems to notice behavior and asks about it and who has well-known, practical sanctions available will seldom need to use them.

The most difficult situation is when such behavior seems to be being encouraged, or at least not discouraged, by executives. This is why it is vital for the leader to be actively building relationships of give-and-take at the executive level in order to support the project, because then the leader can use these relationships to have messages clarified or wayward actions modified.

Does the leader need to make everyone into a "best friend" in order to be successful? No; the situation is well described by Sir John

Harvey-Jones: "You tend to develop friendly acquaintanceships with large numbers of people, develop a few true friends in the real sense, and a few enemies."

Few authors have provided more practical and sage advice for leaders than Herbert Shepard. His rules for change agents help leaders identify "who" to invest time with in building relationships. His advice is as follows:

- Never work uphill: Decide where to invest time based on who is most ready to make meaningful changes for themselves and who will, with guidance, make efficient and effective use of your involvement to get results.

- Find the innovators: Find the people who are willing and able to do the work needed, introduce them to one another, and work with them.

- Light many fires: Start things moving simultaneously in several parts of the organization so that their interactions will tend to reinforce positive change and create momentum.

While the leader plays a crucial role in the short term in both promoting give-and-take and putting ground rules in place and monitoring them, over time it is the credibility generated by stakeholder results that maintains aligned behavior. We explore that topic next.

HOW CREDIBILITY CAN ALIGN BEHAVIOR

A significant challenge for a leader is to manage the credibility of the project. Consultant Dean Meyer described credibility as "the currency of success." His studies of what made projects successful revealed that leaders who knew how to build credibility and use it appropriately had a much higher success rate than those who did not. Credibility for a leader is a track record of projects that provided tangible benefits to their stakeholders. It stands to reason that if any of those stakeholders get a call from a leader whose project has delivered value to them, the call will likely be returned promptly. If a leader needs the participation of stakeholders who have not dealt with him or her before, he or she must communicate previous results to get attention and also leverage collaborative alliances with others who do have credibility with those stakeholders in order to gain their cooperation.

What are the ground rules of credibility? We must examine the findings of Dean Meyer's research. After studying project success, he formulated a game to teach leaders what credibility was and how not to misuse it. In his brochure explaining his game, Meyer quotes *CIO* magazine as having aptly described the game as dealing with "Lessons of the Machiavellian, not microprocessor, kind."

The rules of credibility that Meyer used in his simulations were as follows. At the start of the project a leader has a certain number of credibility chips, representing the credibility built up over the past five years within the organization. When a leader asks for resources, requests people's trust or uses people's time, they use up credibility chips. When they create value indirectly or directly, they gain credibility chips. Indirect value is gained by increasing people's awareness of stakeholder needs so that others take more productive actions to meet them. Direct value is produced through the project's satisfying the felt needs of stakeholders. Any actions that are essential to overall project success but do not create direct stakeholder value must, wherever possible, be conducted in such a way that they create at least indirect value. If a leader uses up credibility faster than they create value, their credibility may run out and then the project is dead, unless rescued by a new leader with large reserves of credibility.

In Meyer's game, players had credibility "chips" (Las Vegas style) and 12 cards to play in whatever sequence they chose. The cards represented different types of action that could be taken to implement IT systems, from carrying out a pilot for key users to drafting an information technology white paper. In line with the maxim that nothing is free, Meyer had players put in credibility chips in order to play their card; it literally cost credibility in order to staff a project or even to get people to attend a meeting.

Similarly, the players received credibility chips as payoffs from cards played in previous rounds. But there was a catch. Players quickly found out that, depending on which order they played their cards, their efforts could quickly grind to a halt because they had run out of credibility chips. This left them holding action cards in their master plan that they could not afford to play. This rang bells with players because they could all recall individuals who had started their new corporate jobs busily and then seemed suddenly to be stranded on the sidelines, no longer even attempting to get anything done. The players realized that these people had run out of credibility and that this made them invisible in the organization. What Meyer's game taught executives was that unless you continuously carry out projects that benefit specific people, who then award you credibility, you will fail. In other words, make sure that you create win-win projects with specific individuals and groups as well as trying to create a win-win for the organization as a whole.

EXAMPLE OF CREDIBILITY OF RESULTS ALIGNING STAKEHOLDER BEHAVIOR

One of the most influential studies of workplace productivity during the 20th century focused on a coal mine in northern England in the late 1940s. The study gave rise to a whole movement, called sociotechnical work systems, that changed the way some organizations viewed the introduction of technology into the workplace. It demonstrates that using give-and-take in the design of the workplace dramatically influences the effectiveness of the outcomes.

In 1949 a postgraduate student at London's Tavistock Institute revisited his former workplace, the coal mine in northern England. What he discovered there led to a whole new way of looking at working relationships. His name was Ken Bamforth and he had been a miner for 18 years before attending university. He and his professor, Eric Trist, went on to research what had happened in the mine and published a landmark book on the subject.

What had occurred was that new technology had been introduced, in the form of improved "roof control," but the mine's general manager had, instead of determining new manning arrangements himself, allowed the men, with union support, to propose their own.

Trist describes what they observed in the mine:

The work organization of the new seam consisted of a set of relatively autonomous groups interchanging roles and shifts and regulating their affairs with a minimum of supervision. Cooperation between task groups was everywhere in evidence, personal commitment was obvious, absenteeism low, accidents infrequent, productivity high. The contrast was large between the atmosphere and arrangements on these faces and those in the conventional areas of the mine where the negative characteristics of the industry were glaringly apparent. The men told us that in order to adapt with the best advantage to the technical conditions in the new seam, they had evolved a form of work organization based on practices common in un-mechanized days (pick and shovels), when small groups, who took responsibility for the entire work cycle had worked autonomously.

In the terms we have been using so far in this book, the mine manager and employees had set ground rules for the conduct of the work to meet stakeholder needs and purposes. The results of implementing these ground rules were improvements in productivity and absenteeism, results that were credible to the stakeholders in the mine, including the national authority overseeing the mines.

The reason that this discovery was so startling was that the prevailing wisdom for most of the 20th century was that of "productivity through technology." In other words, implementing technology and fitting people's roles so as to always operate the technology at maximum utilization gave optimum results. This had meant that the key working relationship for any worker was with the machine they operated. People, according to the theory, no longer needed a relationship with their colleagues, each was merely a cog in a machine.

Trist and Bamforth's research, and the numerous studies that succeeded theirs, showed that the optimum results were obtained by jointly optimizing the technology with the social system or work arrangements and the psychological needs for meaningful work.

Trist and colleagues could be forgiven for believing that a new age was dawning in industrial productivity and harmony. Armed with their step-by-step guide on how to achieve an optimized work system, they went to other mines and tried to implement "the new way." In spite of the fact that the national authority overseeing all British mines supported their efforts, Trist met with very limited success.

The unfortunate issue that Trist encountered was that in order to develop purposes that meet all stakeholder needs and ground rules for give-and-take, one must first get credible people to support and participate in this work. In many cases the notion of give-and-take raises anxieties in the minds of managers, who believe that nothing but anarchy will result.

In spite of an impressive body of research and the collective experience of many organizations on every continent, the mind-set of "technology first" or, as Trist named it, the "technology imperative," has put down deep roots in our thinking and has a broad following, even today. One only has to consider the widely prevailing approach to implementing large ERP computer systems (enterprise resource planning systems) to see the truth of this.

To many people technology is the ultimate instrument for creating order and logic, and therefore give-and-take with employees (or customers) is not to be countenanced lest chaos ensue.

EXAMPLE OF ALIGNING STAKEHOLDER BEHAVIOR: A SCHOOL

A more contemporary example of how a leader can achieve results through give-and-take in planning comes from the story of a school. When Steve Morrison took over as head teacher of Kingsdale School in London, it was a failing school with poor exam results, an appalling truancy rate, low staff morale, and a culture of bullying among students.

But Morrison believed that things could be improved. One particular incident give him cause to hope.

A student was running off of school property, pursued by a teacher. The teacher slipped and fell; the student turned back to check that the teacher was okay before continuing his escape. Says Morrison, "I knew then that there was something to work with."

With Morrison's leadership and teacher support, a project was initiated to revitalize Kingsdale School.

A project team, funded by the national government, took a "whole school" approach, looking at everything from the curriculum to the school management, the staff structure, pastoral care, and issues such as bullying and truancy. This included, crucially, the school buildings themselves: the school yard, cafeteria, washrooms, and classrooms.

They asked students, teachers, and parents what they thought needed to be improved and how best to do it. Then they worked with architects and designers to develop the new-look school, allowing students to choose color schemes and designs.

A key factor was to bring in a curriculum more suited to the aptitudes and ambitions of the students—in other words, more job-related skills.

A key to tackling truancy was felt to be keeping students on-site during lunch breaks. The solution was to create a cafeteria serving popular food and to show movies in the auditorium at lunchtime.

The results have been impressive. Kingsdale's students in national examinations have improved dramatically from 16 percent gaining straight A's to 41 percent. Morale has improved and teachers are now volunteering to give extra help to students after school, something unheard of a few years ago. In a school where students used to run wild, whole classes now stand up when a teacher enters the room.

This is a testimony to the power of give-and-take.

USING THE RULES OF CREDIBILITY TO IMPACT PROJECT RESULTS: RED ADAIR AND THE KUWAIT OIL WELLS

As an example of how leaders can use their credibility to great effect to get an organization to conduct a review and take action, we can find no more striking case than the incident of Red Adair and the Kuwait oil well fires. After the Gulf War in 1991 the oil wells in Kuwait were on fire, set ablaze by retreating troops. The government of Kuwait called in experts from all over the world to help put the fires out. One of those who answered the call was Red Adair, a legendary veteran of numerous difficult well projects. Such was his fame with both oil companies and the public that he had even had a movie made of his life story starring the western star John Wayne. Alas, all did not go smoothly in the project. Adair, seeing that things were off track, decided to take action.

The government forecast that the fires would be put out within a year and full production restored. Then the controversy started. A major newspaper headline (by Christopher Walker in *The Times*) appeared: "Five years to cap oil wells, Adair says."

Red Adair, a 76-year-old who had put out more difficult oil well fires than anyone else, had spoken to reporters about his prediction. He quoted long delays in acquiring equipment, cutting through red tape, and shortages. He claimed that only one-fifth of the equipment ordered had been received, and he accused Kuwaitis of penny-pinching and failing to order equipment early enough.

A flurry of activity followed the publicity around Adair's forecast. Contracts were signed, resources were put in place, and bottlenecks were removed. In due course all the fires were put out, well within the government's forecast.

One interpretation is that the government's plan was on track all along and Adair was just seeking publicity. A more likely interpretation is that the government's plan worked out because Adair spoke out about delays, most of which were under control of the Kuwaiti government. It is quite possible that senior government figures were unaware of the impact that the staff's negotiating tactics had on getting the job done.

What made the changes possible was Adair's credibility, as someone that all the world's oil companies called when an oil well was out of control. He was also known as a plain speaker whose focus was on getting the job done, with safety an overriding priority.

So Adair's credibility focused the minds of decision makers and got them to take action. Nothing succeeds like success.

He spent some of the credibility that he had amassed over decades of successful results. Did he recoup credibility? Perhaps not, but at 76 he probably felt that he had enough left in the credibility bank to do anything else he still needed to do.

USING THE RULES OF CREDIBILITY TO IMPROVE WORKPLACE COMMUNICATION

Meyer's rules of credibility also give us an insight into the common failure of programs intended to get supervisors and employees talking to one another about employees' on-the-job behavior. A common approach is to launch a large project to create and implement a standardized feedback system, usually under the leadership of a human resources executive. This system is by nature people-intensive and meeting-intensive. As a result, many such projects fail because the project and the leader run out of credibility. They go too long without creating value. In fact, it is worse than that. As soon as the project's credibility goes down, fewer people participate, which lowers credibility even faster. An alternative approach, focused on asking people to do less but getting a small payback of credibility immediately, seems to work better. This method, pioneered by Tom Davis, conforms to Meyer's rules of credibility, although that is not how he developed his process. As an entrepreneur and industrial automation enthusiast, he took a problem-solving approach to identify root causes of this lack of communication and came to a surprising conclusion.

In the 1980s, Davis, a Canadian, ran a firm that was a contractor for McDonnell Douglas Aerospace on special aeronautics projects and was invited to participate in the company's "quality-circles" initiative. After two years and many dollars, the program was judged a failure—people hadn't gone to the meetings. Davis became intrigued to understand what was going wrong. His experience with early PCs and industrial automation led him to analyze the communication process among people in the workplace and to contrast Japanese with Western cultural behaviors.

This set him on the trail of finding a practical way to un-block direct communication between employee and supervisor, which he realized was "pivotal" and yet was a link that most companies neglected or even unconsciously undermined. The first version of his tool, the Workplace Communicator, was used by the manager of a Canadian Tire store in 1991 with dramatic results.

The results were so successful and the idea so powerful that Davis left the engineering field altogether and spent the next decade developing, using, and understanding workplace communications.

During face-to-face meetings of about 20 minutes, the employee and supervisor discuss and rate the employee's behavior on 14 topics listed on Workplace Communicator, representing key workplace behaviors, attitudes, and practices. Each employee receives an individualized report.

What Davis found is that repeated cycles of the process (discussion, rating, compilation of scores, reflection) creates momentum for positive change. The process is so simple that everyone has the opportunity to be successful, and having tasted success, to work to maintain it. He says, "Most employees strive to reach the highest standards set in the fourteen topics because they are reachable." The regular face-to-face meetings, with his or her supervisor, provide a framework for better communication and understanding that leads to greater mutual trust.

Supervisors themselves are similarly motivated to change a few key areas of their behavior by going through the same process with their manager. In this case the discussion is enriched with data on the supervisor aggregated from feedback submitted by all the supervisor's employees.

The success cycle is observed by the head of the organization, who sees a report of all the data in the cycle and so knows the extent of participation and the extent of "improvement" and "stretch" taking place throughout the organization. The head can then use his or her own behavior and actions to reinforce the positive progress.

The lesson of Tom Davis and his efforts to improve communication in the workplace is that feedback should not be a complex, once-a-year event between two people that is dreaded beforehand and forgotten afterwards but should be a simple, ongoing process that positively impacts both the individuals involved and the environment (this is why Davis nicknames his process "culture corrector"). People participate a little, see a consequence, participate more, see more consequence, and so on. This is the essence of Meyer's rules of credibility.

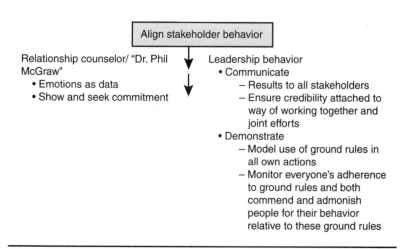

Figure 17.2 Summary of Influence step 3.

SUMMARY

The third and final part of the Influence theme is the aligning of stakeholder behavior. It involves:

- Modeling personal behavior on the ground rules and monitoring stakeholder behavior against them. Bring any significant departures to the notice of those involved.

- Ensuring that the results and smoother working environment are correctly attributed to the jointly defined and supported ground rules. A steady stream of successes is needed to maintain credibility of the relationships. This is described by the saying, "Nothing succeeds like success."

18

Case Study: Using the Leadership Model to Understand Past Failures and Create Future Successes

By centralizing process and distributing the ownership (of decisions) we got the best of both worlds. If people weren't involved in building the forecast and in having input into what was realistic and attainable, we weren't going to get where we needed to be.

Paula Barbary Shannon,
winner of international best sales executive award,
New York, 2004

SOMETIMES A MANAGEMENT TEAM IS ITS OWN WORST ENEMY

Although a critical aspect of leadership concerns individual actions and decisions, management team leadership behavior is very influential. Such aligned purposes, decisions, and behavior can facilitate major changes in an organization.

The executive team of a medium-sized Canadian company was preparing for its annual management meeting, where they planned to officially launch a large process reengineering initiative consisting of a number of subprojects, each scoped to look at a key business process, redesign it, and implement this new design in a phased approach.

The executives felt good about the initiative, which was aimed at implementing the company's new business strategy. As a national supplier of products and service to Canadian businesses, the company had seen its market change with the entry of large U.S.-based competitors who had far greater volumes and a lower cost base. This had driven down profit margins, which had traditionally been in double digits, to single digits.

The company had always focused on providing excellent service and now decided to go more formally into the service business by providing a range of value-added services to its major customers that would save them money. This, it was hoped, would provide a lower total cost solution to customers even when the company was not the cheapest for every item supplied.

The teams had been set up with very capable people and had been trained and had started work already.

The executives very much wanted the managers to understand and support the effort. The company was highly decentralized, and so the local managers had a large degree of autonomy. Consequently if they didn't buy into the initiative it would surely fail.

The business case for the change was solid; the team had the numbers and trends to show the organization. The market was getting tougher, margins were declining, and the company simply had to implement value-added services in addition to its traditional products. Each manager would recognize this based on their own local knowledge. What was bothering the team was something else. The executive team had received feedback from several managers that this new initiative was seen as another "flavor of the month."

The team decided that they just had to deal with this issue somehow if they were to give the new initiative a chance of success. To do so required an acknowledgement that not all the past projects had been successful and the demonstration of a commitment to learn from the successes and failures alike to ensure that this new initiative would be a success.

DEVISING A SIMPLE SURVEY TO GET FEEDBACK

The team concluded that they should devise a simple survey. It would list 12 of the past projects, and each manager would be asked to anonymously rate its success or failure. A one-page survey was designed, giving the managers a five-point scale to check for each project, ranging from "nothing happened/wasted resources" to "all stated goals achieved."

On the first morning of the conference, the 70 or so managers were given a few minutes to think about the 12 projects and rate them, with reasons. Because of the simple design, the results were compiled the same morning and fed back to the group.

The degree of consensus within the group was startling. The same four or five projects were rated as successful, and the same four or five projects as very unsuccessful.

The reasons were widely agreed upon. From analyzing the managers' feedback, it become evident that the successful projects had followed a three-phase approach. Unsuccessful projects had missed one or more steps. In general the more aspects they missed, the less successful they were. They matched the three themes of Intentions, Influence, and Information very closely.

The first phase involved setting clear business objectives, with clear links to customer and company needs and communicating these from the highest level. As one survey respondent expressed it, executives made these successful projects a "companywide must do" and personally communicated their importance to each part of the organization. This was the Intentions theme.

INFLUENCE: USING GIVE-AND-TAKE IN PROJECT ROLL-OUT

The second phase was concerned with creating and implementing a realistic joint roll-out plan between the head office, regional offices, and branch offices. This was the Influence theme and involved planning the roll-out and coming up with a realistic schedule that fit with the unit's business operations based on when they said that they could accommodate the work. It required putting together materials and training that would really help the organization implement the project and assigning responsibilities and support resources to ensure that roll-out would be facilitated and supported. In particular it called for the designation of local point-people who could give information, coordinate work on-site before implementation, and provide first-line support in the crucial period after the company specialists had left.

The assigned facilitators would go to a site at the pre-arranged time and start by giving an overview of why they were there, answering questions, and setting agreed ground rules for the session. The implementation was structured but had room to accommodate local needs, and the facilitators and specialists were prepared to discuss local issues and work through real examples to bring home the importance and the practicality of the new system or program. Generally the managers' feedback suggested that such sessions were enjoyed by staff in the successful projects. During the sessions, individual and unit goals were set for implementing the new system or program with clear measures. After the initial roll-out, further dedicated support was available to answer questions and provide help and advice.

The third phase was the Information theme. This involved a review with each unit and individual who had goals for implementation to see how they had got on. It seems that the most important aspect of the review was that it happened at all. The fact that there was follow-up gave a strong message to people that the company was serious about this project and had not forgotten about it.

It is amazing how often company head offices appear to forget about projects that were promoted as the most important thing in the world only a few weeks before. Why? Because they have moved on to the next project. It is like a movie theater that last week was promoting *Spiderman* as the greatest film of the year and this week is saying the same thing about the latest *Harry Potter*.

In these reviews, line managers asked their direct reports to explain what had been happening. What had been achieved? What had not gone well? What further help did they need; what needed to be adjusted in the program roll-out to improve it? This reinforced the importance of the project and created accountability and consistency within the organization. This review, in the successful cases, was conducted by the unit's boss, not by a head-office specialist (although the specialist may provide data and participate).

THE BIGGEST LESSON FOR THE MANAGEMENT TEAM

The lessons evident in this simple survey had a marked impact on the managers and on the executive team. Although nothing in the data came as a surprise, there was a sense of overall understanding that gave rise to new optimism. There was optimism because at last they realized that they knew the secrets of success; it wasn't a random thing, and they were not cursed or incompetent. When they followed their own best practices, things turned out well, and when they didn't, they failed.

Thus the initiative was launched and with it the new projects. These projects were carefully managed to limit their impact on the organization until it came time for implementation. During the design phase of each project, a wide range of people were interviewed for a short time to "spread the burden" and create greater involvement. The executive team set themselves a rule never to implement more than three projects across the organization at any one time.

For the executive team, this realization had some difficult implications. It meant that all projects needed to receive adequate and realistic resources, implying that far fewer should now be attempted. This led to energetic debate by the executive team on the company's real priorities: the projects that had to be done and, most difficult of all, the projects that had to wait.

For perhaps the first time in its history, the company's executive team chose to hold off on implementing projects. It was tough to do, with new versions of software and new products that were beneficial things in themselves. But the team knew that unless they focused the organization and did a proper job of following the phased approach inherent in the leadership model, none of their projects would achieve targeted benefits.

SUMMARY

This case of a Canadian company launching a vital process reengineering project shows:

- Analyzing the history of a company's projects with an open mind usually reveals that an inconsistent approach to leadership is behind many of the failures.

- The leadership model of Intentions, Influence, and Information can be used as a planning and diagnostic tool to increase the chances of an initiative being successful and achieving targeted benefits.

19

Key Questions for Leaders

It's never too late to be what you might have been.
Mary Ann Evans
(better known as 19th-century British author George Eliot)

A STRATEGY FOR GETTING STARTED

What advice do we offer to leaders who wish to use the ideas in this book?

Edward De Bono describes gaining an understanding of something as a process of changing the unfamiliar into the familiar, by thinking, so that you know what to do about it. With that in mind there are two main types of "next steps."

If the main arguments we have offered so far have resonated with you at all, start to apply the model. Learn from observing what happens. Reread the sections that you find most difficult to apply.

If the whole model is still foggy and your head is swimming with data, put the book aside for a couple of weeks and come back to it later. In the meantime, pay careful attention to the dynamics going on around you. Where do you see and hear intentions made clear, influence brought to bear, and information leveraged effectively? And where are those noticeably absent? Do you see a difference in results between these two situations? If yes, reread the book with your own examples in mind.

Then there are natural questions that arise, such as:

- Don't I need to understand this model completely before attempting to use it?

- Aren't there contingency factors, situations that dictate a certain style of action is more appropriate?

First, understanding things thoroughly at the detailed level is good but not always necessary. If you've grasped the main points and are sufficiently convinced of its lack of risk and high return, it's better to learn and improve by doing. In this sense your leadership impact on the organization is like a "black box"; you know what you must do to trigger the right things to occur and you don't necessarily need to worry about the exact cause and effect that goes on around you in a dynamic environment.

The contingency issue is more of a "how" issue. Researchers such as Fred Fiedler have argued that leader effectiveness depends on the interaction between situation and leadership style. In particular, it depends on the preexisting relationship (especially credibility), relative clarity of the situation or task facing the organization, and the positional power of the leader relative to others. Few could argue that these are vital factors.

However, in considering the model we've outlined, the only thing that changes is the "how," not the "what" or "why." For instance, a leader setting out to identify stakeholder needs in a team meeting may get up and move to a flipchart, whereas in their boss's management meeting they would use a different approach. In that meeting, the leader might say, "I see the customer has been considered, but just so that I'm clear, who else should we be consulting on this project?"

The most common problem around involvement is that leaders don't know when to involve themselves and when not to. They may wish to involve themselves yet fear it will eat up time and set expectations that they can't sustain. In this work we advocate three crucial

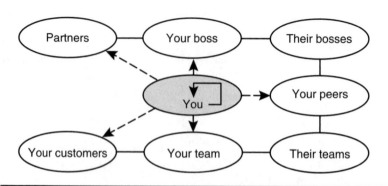

Figure 19.1 Looking for points of highest leverage.

areas of involvement: purposes, behavioral ground rules, and reviews of performance. Everything else is an option. A contingency framework such as Fiedler's will help leaders make more optimal judgments about these other situations.

Assuming that you are ready to think about where to start your application, here are some questions that might help you identify the areas of greatest potential payback.

One framework for this analysis is to consider a chessboard analysis. Imagine yourself on a single square surrounded by other chess pieces. In order to impact the organization in any meaningful way, you must first attempt to work with and through three of these pieces, which are fundamental: yourself, your team, and your boss.

Only then can one hope to influence the other parties with whom one has contact, such as customers, peers, and partners.

We can look for points of highest leverage by examining each of the three themes of Intention, Influence, and Information for all of the three key domains: self, team, and boss. To assist with this, here are some questions for self-examination.

INFLUENCE: PROMOTE GIVE-AND-TAKE BEHAVIOR WITHIN YOURSELF

Proactive people focus their efforts on things they can do something about. The nature of their energy is positive. Reactive people on the other hand, focus their efforts on the weaknesses of other people, the problems in the environment and circumstances over which they have no control. This creates negative energy.

Stephen Covey

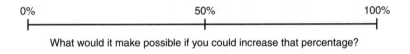

What percentage of the time are you able to avoid focusing energy on things that you cannot do anything about?

0%   50%   100%
├─────────────────────────────┼─────────────────────────────┤

What would it make possible if you could increase that percentage?

Figure 19.2   Influence yourself.

INFLUENCE: PROMOTE GIVE-AND-TAKE BEHAVIOR WITHIN YOUR TEAM

I come to you with an idea that you think is very good, but rather than just saying, "great idea," your tendency, because you have to win, is to say, "good idea, but do it this way." Well you might have improved the quality of my idea 5% but you've reduced my commitment to executing it by 30% because you took away my ownership. One of my clients who is now a CEO at a major company said that he got into the habit of taking a breath before he talked, and realized that about half of what he was going to say wasn't worth saying. Even though he thought he was right, he realized he had more to gain by not "winning."

Marshall Goldsmith

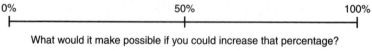

Approximately how much of what you say is really aimed at improving the outcome, versus making yourself feel or look better?

| 0% | 50% | 100% |

What would it make possible if you could increase that percentage?

Figure 19.3   Influence your team.

INFLUENCE: PROMOTE GIVE-AND-TAKE BEHAVIOR WITH YOUR BOSS

In response to "we just can't do that," instead of asking "why," try saying "because if we did . . . ?"

This gives us a different kind of answer. The answer to a why question is a rational defense or excuse. Such an approach helps us not only understand (our boss), but also helps both of us think more clearly about management issues.

Joann Chenault

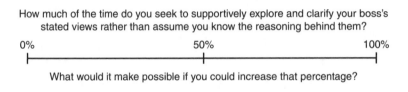

How much of the time do you seek to supportively explore and clarify your boss's stated views rather than assume you know the reasoning behind them?

0%   50%   100%

What would it make possible if you could increase that percentage?

Figure 19.4   Influence your boss.

INTENTION: PROMOTE STAKEHOLDER-FOCUSED THINKING IN YOURSELF

Set aside five minutes of the day for a deliberate wearing of the thinking hat. For instance one person said, "I thought it was silly and artificial because I knew what I thought. But when I had done it, I found that my mind was changed by what I, myself, had written down."

It depends on whether you believe you are paid to think or (merely) follow the thinking of others.

Edward De Bono

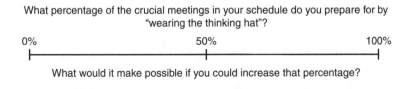

What percentage of the crucial meetings in your schedule do you prepare for by "wearing the thinking hat"?

0%   50%   100%

What would it make possible if you could increase that percentage?

Figure 19.5   Intention: Yourself.

INTENTION: PROMOTE STAKEHOLDER-FOCUSED THINKING WITHIN YOUR TEAM

Most organizations lack the discipline to figure out with ego-less clarity what they can be the best at, and the will to do whatever it takes to turn that potential into reality.

In this regard, "stop-doing" lists are more important than "to-do" lists.

Jim Collins

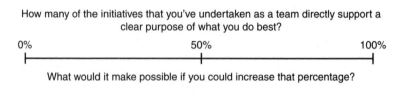

How many of the initiatives that you've undertaken as a team directly support a clear purpose of what you do best?

0%   50%   100%

What would it make possible if you could increase that percentage?

Figure 19.6   Intention: Your team.

INTENTION: PROMOTE STAKEHOLDER-FOCUSED THINKING IN YOUR BOSS

Intangible assets seldom have value by themselves (brand names, which can be sold, are an exception). Generally, intangible assets must be bundled to create value. For example a new growth oriented sales strategy could require new knowledge about customers, new training for sales employees, new databases, new information systems, a new organization structure, and a new incentive compensation program.

Investing in just one of these capabilities, or in all of them but one, would cause the new sales strategy to fail. To measure [the benefit of investing in] these assets we need to identify cause-and-effect linkages [using, for example, the balanced scorecard and strategy map] to describe how intangible assets get mobilized and combined with other assets to deliver customer value propositions and desired financial outcomes.

Robert Kaplan and David Norton

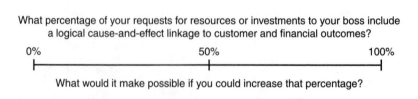

What percentage of your requests for resources or investments to your boss include a logical cause-and-effect linkage to customer and financial outcomes?

0%   50%   100%

What would it make possible if you could increase that percentage?

Figure 19.7   Intention: Your boss.

INFORMATION: PROMOTE DATA-BASED DECISIONS WITH YOURSELF

Whenever you make a key decision or take a key action, write down what you expect will happen. Later compare the actual results with your expectation. Practiced consistently, this simple method will show where your strengths lie, which is the most important thing to know. Put yourself where your strengths can produce results. Work on improving your strengths by improving skills and acquiring new ones.

Peter Drucker

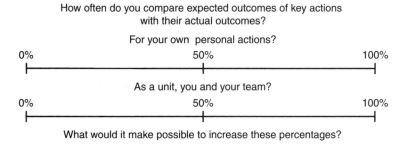

How often do you compare expected outcomes of key actions with their actual outcomes?

For your own personal actions?

| 0% | 50% | 100% |

As a unit, you and your team?

| 0% | 50% | 100% |

What would it make possible to increase these percentages?

Figure 19.8   Information: Yourself.

INFORMATION: PROMOTE DATA-BASED DECISIONS WITH YOUR TEAM

Resistance [to change], instead of a force to be ignored or wiped out, was seen by Kurt Lewin as a source of energy needing constructive outlets. Lewin's philosophy called for all the people who are key to implementation to wrestle with the data together and arrive at a mutually acceptable action plan. This involves multiple realities, the views of several people, not simply those of experts, or top management, or supervisors, or workers, or customers, or suppliers, but all those whose information is relevant.

Lewin saw the process as a never-ending one, based on trial, error, feedback, and learning. He was especially scathing about managers who delegate one-shot change projects.

Marvin Weisbord

What percentage of the "improvement actions" generated by your team arise from the involvement of stakeholders who have all wrestled with the appropriate data?

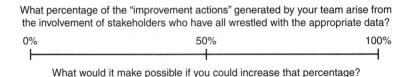

What would it make possible if you could increase that percentage?

Figure 19.9   Information: Your team.

INFORMATION: PROMOTE DATA-BASED DECISIONS WITH YOUR BOSS

A community extends only as far as the effective transmission of information. Unity is achieved in self-organizing systems through each member both transmitting and receiving information. Which due to the natural phenomenon of "attraction" of frequencies in the nervous systems, means that communities converge to "broadcasting" on a common frequency. In this way a colony of fireflies in a tree is seen to be flashing in unison.

Norbert Wiener

To what extent have you been able to include your boss in your community by keeping him or her in your team's communication loop?

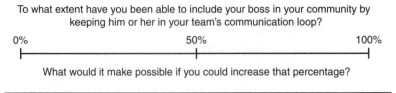

What would it make possible if you could increase that percentage?

Figure 19.10   Information: Your boss.

ON YOUR JOURNEY

Based on your answers to these questions, you can probably see where your top two or three opportunities may be for applying these ideas to your own circumstances.

In the event that a new initiative presents itself to you, you may wish to apply the three I's in each of your interactions to discharge your leadership responsibilities more effectively while using your time more wisely.

As you work with these ideas, feel free to share them with me, via my website, www.leadershipforresults.org, where I will post further information and details of work in progress by those attempting to improve their leadership.

I can think of no better closing line than to quote Tom Mueller's words on the lessons of the Eco-Challenge: "In this world the kind of leadership that leads somewhere is less pushy and totalitarian."

Bibliography

Arter, Dennis, and J. P. Russell. "Ethics, Auditing and Enron." *Quality Progress* (October 2003), pp. 34–40.

Audi, Robert. *Action, Intention, and Reason.* Ithaca, NY: Cornell University Press, 1993.

Barker, Tom. "The Magic Factor: The Critical Role of Sponsorship in Making Projects a Success." *Project Times* (Fall 2002), pp. 3–6.

Bennis, Warren. *Why Leaders Can't Lead.* San Francisco: Jossey-Bass, 1989.

Bennis, Warren, and Burt Nanus. *Leaders.* New York: HarperBusiness, 2003.

Bonabeau, Eric. "The Perils of the Imitation Age." *Harvard Business Review* (June 2004), pp. 45–54.

Brand, Stewart. *How Buildings Learn: What Happens after They're Built.* New York: Viking Penguin Books, 1994.

Brinkley, Douglas G. *The Atlantic Charter.* New York: Palgrave Macmillan, 1994.

Buch, Esteban. *Beethoven's Ninth: A Political History.* Chicago: University of Chicago Press, 2003.

Burg, Jerry. "Learning from Columbia." *Quality Progress* (March 2004).

BusinessWeek Online. "Best and Worst Managers of the Year." (January 10, 2005).

Chenault, Joann. "The Grammar of Consulting." *Journal of Management Consulting* 7(2) (Fall 1992), pp. 56–57.

Cherrington, J. Owen. "Observation: It Helps to Know Your Beans." *Journal of Management Consulting* 7(2) (Fall 1992), pp. 48–49.

Clugston, Michael. "The Fast Trackers." *Canadian Geographic Magazine* (July/August 2002), pp. 78–82.

Collins, James. *Good to Great: Why Some Companies Make the Leap and Others Don't.* New York: HarperCollins, 2001.

Collins, James, and Jerry Porras. *Built to Last.* New York: HarperCollins, 1997.

Conan Doyle, Sir Arthur. *The Adventures of Sherlock Holmes.* Ware, UK: Words Worth Editions, 1992.

Cooper, Robert R., and Sawaf Ayman. *Executive EQ: Emotional Intelligence in Leadership and Organizations.* New York: Perigree/Penguin, 1997.

Covey, Stephen R. *The 7 Habits of Highly Effective People: Restoring the Character Ethic.* Toronto: Free Press, 1989.

Cribb, Robert, and Tyler Hamilton. "How a Giant Fell to Earth." *The Toronto Star* (December 8, 2001).

Davis, Tom. "The WorkPlace Communicator," www.pivotalrelationships.com, June 2005.

Dawkins, Richard. *The Selfish Gene.* New York: Oxford University Press, 1989.

De Bono, Edward. *Six Thinking Hats.* Toronto: Little, Brown, 1985.

De Geus, Arie. "The Living Company." *Harvard Business Review* (March–April 1997), pp. 51–59.

"Definitions of Job Titles." *Quality Progress* (December 2003).

Deming, Edwards W. *Out of Crisis: Quality, Productivity and Competitive Position.* Cambridge, MA: Cambridge University Press, 1986.

Dixon, Norman. *On the Psychology of Military Incompetence.* London: Pimlico Random House, 1994.

Drucker, Peter F. "Managing Oneself." *Harvard Business Review* (January 2005).

———. "What Makes an Effective Executive?" *Harvard Business Review* (June 2004), pp. 58–63.

Dudash, Robin. "Software Stakeholder Management: It's Not All It's Coded Up to Be." *Software Quality* 2 (Spring 2003), pp. 1, 4–6.

Dvorak, Phred, and Merissa Marr. "Sony Confirms Foreigner as CEO; Tough Decisions to Be on Agenda." *Wall Street Journal* story published in Toronto *Globe and Mail* (March 8, 2005).

Eccles, Robert G., Nitin Nohria, and James D. Berkley. *Beyond the Hype: Rediscovering the Essence of Management.* Boston: Harvard Business School Press, 1992.

Fiedler, F. E. "Situational Control and a Dynamic Theory of Leadership." In K. Grint (ed.). *Leadership: Classical, Contemporary and Critical Approaches.* Oxford, UK: Oxford University Press, 1997.

Finkelstein, Sydney. *Why Smart Executives Fail, and What You Can Learn from Their Mistakes.* New York: Portfolio/Penguin, 2003.

Fornari, Arthur, and George Maszle. "Xerox Learns Six Sigma." *Six Sigma Forum Magazine* (August 2004).

Gallwey, Timothy W. *The Inner Game of Tennis.* Toronto: Bantam Books, 1979.

Garvin, David A. "The Processes of Organization and Management." *Sloan Management Review* (Summer 1998), pp. 33–50.

Garvin, David A., and Michael A. Roberto. "Change through Persuasion." *Harvard Business Review* (February 2005).

Goldsmith, Marshall. "Behave Yourself: A Conversation with Executive Coach Marshall Goldsmith." *Harvard Business Review* (October 2002), pp. 22–24.

Hall, Amanda. "Working Title Rolls the Dice for U.S. $50 Million." *Financial Post* (April 9, 2001).

Hartley-Brewer, Julia. "A Model School for the 21st Century." *The International Express* (December 31, 2002).

Harvey-Jones, John. *Trouble Shooter 2.* London: BBC Books, 1992.

Harvey-Jones, John. *Sir John Harvey Jones in His Own Words.* (Audio recording.) Red Audio, www.redaudio.biz, 2002.

Hershberg, Jerry. *The Creative Priority: Putting Innovation to Work in Your Business.* New York, Harper Business, 1998.

Hiebeler, Robert, Thomas B. Kelly, and Charles Ketteman. *Best Practices: Building Your Business with Customer-Focused Solutions.* New York: Simon & Schuster, 1998.

Janis, I. L, *Victims of Groupthink.* Boston: Houghton Mifflin, 1972.

Kaplan, Robert S., and David R. Norton. *The Strategy Focused Organization: How Balanced Scorecard Companies Thrive in the New Business Environment.* Boston: Harvard Business School Press, 2001.

———. *Strategy Maps: Converting Intangible Assets into Tangible Outcomes.* Boston, Harvard Business School Press. 2004.

Kim, Y. *Universal Ethics: From the Perspective of Religious Traditions. Sitges Catalunya* UNESCO Universal Ethics Project, October 7–10, 1998.

Kotter, John P. "What Effective General Managers Really Do." *Harvard Business Review* (March 1, 1999).

Lencioni, Patrick. *The Five Dysfunctions of a Team: A Leadership Fable.* San Francisco: Jossey-Bass, Wiley, 2002.

Levy, David H., "Arthur C. Clarke's Vision of the Cosmos," *Sky and Telescope Magazine,* May 2001, pp. 80–81.

Lovell, Jim, and Jeffrey Kluger. *Apollo 13: Lost Moon.* Toronto: Pocket Books, 1995.

Lowe, Janet. *Warren Buffet Speaks: Wit and Wisdom from the World's Greatest Investor.* Toronto: John Wiley & Sons, 1997.

Lukacs, John. *The Duel: 10 May–31 July 1940, The Eighty-Day Struggle Between Churchill and Hitler.* New York: Ticknor and Fields, 1991.

Martin, Michael H. "The Man Who Makes Sense of Numbers." *Fortune* (October 27, 1997).

McLuhan, Marshall, and Quentin Fiore. *The Medium Is the Message.* New York: Touchstone, 1967.

Meyer, N. Dean. "Gameplan," www.ndma.com, June 2005.

Mintzberg, Henry. "Enough Leadership." *Harvard Business Review* (November 2004), p. 24.

Morton, Keith. "When Things Go Wrong." *Explore Magazine* (May/June 2000), pp. 61–63.

Mueller, Tom. "Eco-Trippers." *Hemispheres Magazine* (April 1998).

Nadler G., S. Hibino, and J. Farrell. *Creative Solution Finding.* Rocklin, CA: Prima Publishing, 1995.

Pirsig, Robert. *Zen and the Art of Motorcycle Maintenance: An Inquiry into Values.* New York: HarperCollins, 1974.

Rackham N., and John Carlisle. "The Effective Negotiator—Part 1: The Behaviour of Successful Negotiators." *Journal of European Industrial Training* 2(6) (1978), pp. 6–10.

Ryan, Sr. Mary Jean. "Process Design and Management: The Path to Organizational Transformation." *Journal of Innovative Management* (Summer 2000), pp. 51–64.

Schlager, Neil. *Breakdown: Deadly Technological Disasters.* Detroit: Visible Ink Press, 1995.

Senge, Peter M. *The Fifth Discipline: The Art and Practices of the Learning Organization.* New York: Doubleday/Currency, 1990.

Shepard, Herbert A. "Rules of Thumb for Change Agents." *Organizational Development Practitioner* (1975), pp. 1–5.

Simon, Herbert A. *The Sciences of the Artificial.* Cambridge, MA: MIT Press, 1996.

Simpson, John. *The Concise Oxford Dictionary of Proverbs.* Oxford, UK: Oxford University Press, 1985.

Slater, Philip, and Warren G. Bennis. "Democracy Is Inevitable." *Harvard Business Review* (March–April 1964).

Small, Hugh. *Florence Nightingale: Avenging Angel.* London: Constable, 1998.

Spindler, Garold R. "Managing in Uncertainty: Lessons from the Underground." *Quality Progress* (January 2001), pp 83–87.

Steward, Donald V. *Systems Analysis and Management: Structure, Strategy and Design.* New York: PBI-Petrocelli Books, 1981.

Taormina, Tom. "From Quality to Business Success." *Quality Progress* (April 2002).

"The Two Row Wampum Treaty Belt and Its Place at the Law Society of Upper Canada." Commemorative Pamphlet. Law Society of Upper Canada, 1998.

Tolkien, J. R. R. *The Silmarillion.* London: HarperCollins, 1997.

Trist, Eric. "The Evolution of Socio-Technical Systems: A Conceptual Framework and an Action Research Program." *Issues in Quality of Working Life* 2 (June 1981). Ontario Quality of Working Life Centre, Ontario Ministry of Labour, pp. 2–11.

Tufte, Edward R. *Visual and Statistical Thinking: Displays of Evidence for Making Decisions.* Cheshire, CT: Graphics Press, 1997.

Walker, Christopher. "Five Years to Cap Oil Wells, Adair Says." *The Times* (London) (June 14, 1991), pp. 1, 20.

Watson, Gregory H., and Peter F. Drucker. "Delivering Value to Customers." *Quality Progress* (May 2002), pp. 55–61.

Weisbord, Marvin R. *Productive Workplaces: Organization and Managing for Dignity, Meaning, and Community.* San Francisco: Jossey-Bass, 1987.

Welch, Jack, with John A. Byrne. *Jack: Straight from the Gut.* New York: Warner Business Books, 2001.

Wheatley, Margaret J. *Leadership and the New Science: Learning about Organization from an Orderly Universe.* San Francisco: Berrett-Koehler, 1992.

Wiener, Norbert. *Cybernetics: Or Control and Communication in the Animal and the Machine.* Cambridge, MA: MIT Press, 1994.

Winston, Patrick Henry. *Artificial Intelligence,* 2nd ed. Reading, MA: Addison-Wesley, 1984.

Wintrob, Suzanne. "Sales Executive Sets Bar High." *Financial Post* (March 29, 2004), pp. 1, 4.

Index